# THE 7 ESSENTIAL ELEMENTS OF IRRESISTIBLE WOMEN

*Why some women get Ghosted, Played, and Manipulated while others are dating quality men and finding healthy relationships*

## VICTORIA KNIGHTLEY

contained within this document, including, but not limited to, errors, omissions, or inaccuracies.

# FREE GIFT FOR MY READERS

If you want to learn more about the 7 most common myths putting a halt on your happiness, enjoy this FREE GIFT FOR MY READERS!

# INTRODUCTION

"Your vision will become clear only when you can look into your own heart. Who looks outside, dreams; who looks inside, awakes."

— CARL JUNG (JUNG, 2011)

I challenge you to open up a romance book or start streaming a romantic movie. Chances are you'll stumble upon a heroine who is somehow pretty amazing (she's good looking, she has a more than decent career, and usually has at somewhat of a sense of humor as well).

And yet, your heroine is most probably single (because nobody starts romance movies and books with a happily married woman, right?). Even more so, your heroine has been heartbroken one too many times and she's now erring on the side of caution when it comes to dating (and rightfully so, let's face it).

Somehow, as if through magic, the heroine ends up with her very own "the one." I'd very much like to say her version of "the one" is hers alone, but the truth is that most times, these works of fiction play around with two or three archetypes and nothing more. As such, the journey of the heroine becomes just a play on specific genre tropes—and not in any way something we can learn from.

Sure, we all love a bit of romantic fiction every now and again and that's perfectly fine. However, drawing your life lessons from such works is bound to yield poor results.

What, then, will actually teach you how to get the man of your dreams?

Is it glossy magazines, maybe?

Well, yes, sure, that can work. But same as romance movies and books, glossy magazines frequently get stuck on stereotypes and cheap tricks. A lot of them are very good and they can teach you a thing or two about empowerment, having a better sex life, or looking your best. But at the end of the day, they mostly fail in delivering the information women need to enhance themselves in a real sense and both attract and keep the man that's good for them.

Notice how I used "for them" here, because it's pretty important. The reason most of the dating advice fails is simple: it does not work with you, nor does it work with the kind of man you want to attract. I prefer to give you clear guidelines and have you fill in the details of how it will best suit you as an individual. There are seven billion people on the planet and nobody could ever fit them in categories that are comprehensive and truthful enough.

What then?

The only solution you have is to take the slightly longer path. It sounds tiresome, I know, but I promise it's going to give you a lot more satisfaction than you even imagine—and not just in your dating life.

Is the book at hand going to help you in your journey?

Absolutely. I cannot promise much because I'm not a fortune teller (nor do I want to lie to you in any way). What I can promise, however, is that this book will reveal to you the secrets, the techniques great women use to attract great men, and the things modern femme fatales do that make them simply irresistible. If you don't think you have a femme fatal just beneath the surface, I look forward to helping you discover her!

Meet the Brilliant Vixen, the concept that has been missing from your life, the link that connects all the good information out there, and the technique that will help you boost yourself to a whole new, improved, absolutely amazing version of your own self.

The Brilliant Vixen is where the "Brilliance" of a woman who is both highly intelligent and shines like a star meets the vixen, another word for a female fox, which is the physical embodiment of sly femininity.

A "Brilliant Vixen" is a woman who looks at dating as a fun adventure, rather than making "finding a man" her sole purpose in life. The Brilliant Vixen refuses to settle for anything less than what she deserves (which is, you guessed it, an amazing man).

This archetype has solid boundaries, and she uses them as her armor to protect her heart from those who would try to steal her happiness. A Brilliant Vixen tends to be extremely focused on what matters to her, yet she maintains a warm and welcoming demeanor. Believe it or not, these traits do not have to be mutually exclusive.

Brilliant Vixens practice compassion as part of their day to day lives, yet their affection is strictly reserved for those who have earned it (which, again, consists of people who are nothing short of exceptional for them).

In this book, I will teach you how to be a Brilliant Vixen—a woman who's fearless, yet sensitive, mysterious, yet open, fun, yet high-value. In other words, I will teach you how to be the kind of woman truly quality men want in their lives.

Keep in mind that you do not have to "become" a Brilliant Vixen in the pure sense of the word. You just have to awaken all these dormant qualities which already exist inside yourself. It might take a little work to bring them to surface and allow them to shine through past histories, trauma, pain, fear, anxieties, and lack of self-esteem.

How exactly does one embrace her Brilliant Vixen?

I have designed a seven-stage system that will help you get *there*, where you need to be to align your vibrations with the vibrations of men who are worth your time, effort, and emotion.

This system is designed to look and "behave" like an iceberg. The first two stages of the Brilliant Vixen system are the tip of the iceberg, the basis for how successful women are at attracting men. It is important for you to keep in mind that *attraction*, in its incipient stage, is just the *tip* of the iceberg.

That means that, if you have no trouble attracting men, but wonder why all your relationships are surface level, it might be because the remaining five elements in your Brilliant Vixen are not as well developed. These last few elements of the metaphor determine how much value men assign to you, so they are obviously crucial.

Let's dive a little deeper into the iceberg metaphor. The first two qualities I will describe in this book are the only ones that are easily perceived, just like the tip of an iceberg. People can tell right away if you're fun or not, and they can also easily tell if you're flirting with them or not. That's just what's easy to see from the surface.

The five remaining qualities are what happens below the surface. Although they cannot be seen with the naked eye, they make up the majority of the "whole" (the iceberg, or, to be more specific, the essence of the Brilliant Vixen). Having these qualities are the ones that fill people with deep respect and admiration for you. It is these characteristics that show you're not an ice cube that can be easily pushed around in a drink, but a **force of nature that commands respect**.

As you will notice in the book, these elements are not necessarily 100% separable from each other. Many of them cross over into each other, and that's exactly how they make each other stronger. Just like Aristotle said, "The whole is greater than the sum of its parts"—and that stands just as true in the case of the Brilliant Vixen iceberg metaphor too.

Keep in mind that these elements do not only affect each other positively, but negatively too. For instance, one bad behavior could negatively affect three or four elements at the same time. As you continue to read on, you'll start to see how well these seven elements compliment each other and how, when combined, they will make you a happier, more fulfilled individual before you even bring another person into the mix.

Being a Brilliant Vixen has nothing to do with emulating qualities men seek in women. But it has everything to do with finding your true self and being a strong woman in the most powerful, yet feminine sense of the word.

Being a Brilliant Vixen is about self-empowerment that boosts your love life, not imitating others to mimic their love life. The seven elements I will describe in this book work no matter who you are, where you come from, what your social status may be, or even what your story might be.

Brilliant Vixens are timeless. They do not submit to the social standards of the 21st century, 18th century, or 9th century. They do not follow standards of beauty that belong to a specific era. They are themselves, their absolute, true selves beyond time, fashion, size, and social expectations.

Yes, men will naturally gravitate towards women they find physically attractive, based on whatever personal criteria they have. Once they've found something attractive in you, however, things have just begun—and being a Brilliant Vixen will help you uncover a true love story, rather than let it sink before it has a chance to flourish.

Women who posses the seven quintessential elements of a Brilliant Vixen are simply happier, and not just because they date better men, but because they:

- Genuinely enjoy the dating process

- Attract more quality matches
- Are happy with who they are, in and outside of their relationships
- Don't settle for anything less than what they actually want

The **best** news about the Brilliant Vixen elements is that they can all be cultivated. Most women are not born to be 100% Brilliant Vixens, but they surely possess the necessary qualities. Some are more fun, but less high-value, others are more mysterious, but not so flirty. If you learn how to work on all the elements to become more balanced, you have won this game.

No matter where you are right now with each of these individual elements, you can always have more. You can always be more.

Why would you believe me, Victoria Knightley? Why would you trust my method, my advice, or even my uplifting words?

Well, to begin with, I am a proud Brilliant Vixen too. I am now happily married to Liam, an amazing man who has been nothing but supportive of me through thick and thin. We currently live in Las Vegas, Nevada, where we raise our wonderful artist daughter, Janis, whom we named after one of our favorite musicians of all time: Janis Joplin.

Our lives are anything but boring because we know how to hold each other to high standards and because we really get each other. We travel the world and get married to each other every year on our anniversary. We've actually gotten married everywhere from the Mayan Pyramid ruins in Belize (where a Maya priest in a Jaguar Headdress married us) to the heart of the New Orleans French Quarter in a romantic ceremony for two. In 2020 we had to roll with the punches but still carried on our tradition by having a quarantine edition ceremony. We got dressed up and got married via Zoom by a Creole friend of ours who's a minister... and a DJ, we do live in Vegas after all.

I want women everywhere to experience the same level of happiness I have. I know that, due to a variety of circumstances, many women are stuck in situations that do not befit them or their true dreams. I've spent time being stuck in relationships that definitely did not suit me and were frankly soul-crushing. Discovering this proven path to happiness and abundance was one of the most enlightening things in my life and I'm incredibly excited to be able to share all of it with you!

My sole purpose with this book is to help you find your path, your own version of the Brilliant Vixen model. I have decided to make a career out of writing about dating and relationships precisely because my research has always yielded great results. I have been actively involved in the Glasser Institute and studied "Choice Theory" for more than a decade, which has helped me develop my own behavioral theories in the dating and relationships niche.

All in all, you should believe me and my method because I have a track record of success in actually helping people (starting with myself and ending with the incredible women who have used my advice and succeeded at being very happy).

I do not claim to hold the ultimate truth, nor would I ever want to claim such things. What I claim and can swear by is my method's ability to bring out the very best in you, so that you can attract the very best that's out there.

No matter who you are, what you do for a living, or what your track record of relationships is, I would absolutely love to see you succeed. Because nothing brings me more joy than knowing my advice helped you wake up every day smiling, truly satisfied with your life from every point of view.

I'm so excited to help you bring your personal Brilliant Vixen to the surface. I know you can do it, and I know what an immense strength it will give you as a woman.

Leave your heartache and self-limiting beliefs at the door and step with me into a life that is happier and more fulfilling than your wildest dreams! The life you deserve!

*Chapter One*

# FUN

---

"I had too much fun was no one's last regret ever."

— JONATHAN HEATT ("A QUOTE BY JONATHAN HEATT," N.D.)

---

Believe it or not, there's nothing funny about wanting to be fun to attract the opposite sex. In fact, it is exactly what you should want.

Being fun is no laughing matter, say scientists, and I tend to agree. It's not even just a matter of attracting the opposite sex. It's a matter of simply living well.

Living surrounded by people and allowing yourself to be at the center of their life too.

In this chapter, we will discuss being fun, having a sense of humor, and how to use these things to attract the men you want in your life. As mentioned in the introduction, this will mark the tip of our iceberg—the first stage of attracting men worth your time and your energy.

Keep in mind: although we might talk about fun, the information in this chapter is not to be taken lightly. Even after the first stages of a relationship, being fun will still account for keeping the fire alive and making sure your man really wants to stay with you, instead of straying away from you.

"When a marriage begins to go sour, fun is the first casualty. That's too bad because fun is the easiest need to satisfy. There are so many things you can do to have fun, and rarely does anyone stand in your way." Dr. Glasser, M.D. from Choice Theory A new Psychology of Personal Freedom

## WHY BEING FUN IS IMPORTANT

Most people take sense of humor lightly. That's perfectly normal, actually. We don't stop to analyze the jokes that make us laugh. Even more, the vast majority of people with a well-developed sense of humor do not necessarily stop to analyze their "funny" either.

If you really do stop to think of it, laughing and being funny are just a little odd. The way the mouth opens to laugh, the way the voice changes to adapt to laughing sounds, how our skin glows and our eyes shine when we are having fun—they seem a little weird, compared to how we behave any other time.

And yet, people need this little "oddity" in their lives. Our brain consistently seeks the chemicals released by fun times: dopamine, serotonin, oxytocin, and endorphins. Each of these is released in different kinds of "feel-good moments," but each of them is equally addictive. These chemicals are the reason we seek people who make us feel good, the reason some people get addicted to running, and the reason we constantly seek instant gratification when binge-watching our favorite Netflix show.

Being fun is far more important than most of us realize. We don't normally list "sense of humor" on our LinkedIn unless we're in a creative niche—but we sure need a sense of humor and the ability to let go and have fun as part of our lives.

Studies show that this starts very early in our lives. For instance, in an experiment run by Florida

Atlantic University and Concordia University in Montreal over two months, researchers showed that fun kids are generally more popular and more liked by their peers. What is perhaps even more interesting than this is that "being fun" was even higher on the list of "criteria" for liking someone than physical attractiveness, athletic ability, or even prosocial behavior. To quote the study authors, "Fun begets status and status begets fun" in an intrinsic relationship visible even in the younger members of society (Galoustian, 2020).

This goes to show that our brains are almost literally wired to seek people who offer us a good time—and that this is not even a social construct, but something deeply embedded in how human beings function.

How about adults? Are they likely as children to let themselves get close to those who are fun?

Of course they are, and you might not even need a study for this. Just think of your own behaviors. Are you more likely to spend time with a coworker who is always a good sport and makes good jokes or a coworker who's always gloomy? Are you more likely to want to spend time with a fun friend on a Saturday night or someone who's just not that interesting? Are you more likely to date a guy who makes you laugh or one who makes you feel nostalgic or downright sad?

Yes, we sometimes have to take the responsibility of spending time with people who are not fun (or at least not in the moment). And yes, life is not always fun. But at the end of the day, being fun and being around people who are fun is a deep need our brain is constantly seeking.

You might think you're well past your childhood and play has no role in your life—but you would be dead wrong. Play is just as important in the lives of adults as it is in those of children, and this is one of the main reasons we always seek-out people who are fun.

There is a very long list of reasons why being fun and playful as an adult is great for you and for those around you:

- It helps you relieve stress (precisely because it helps release feel-good chemicals in the brain)
- It helps your brain stay active and improve its function (including when you partake in fun social activities with family and friends)
- It stimulates your brain and boosts your creativity (and this applies to adult learning as much as it does to childhood learning)
- It helps you connect to others and improve your relationship with them

- It helps you feel young and energized no matter what your ID card might say
- It teaches you how to cooperate with others and improves your social skills in general
- It helps you heal emotional wounds

At work and at home during our leisure time, the benefits of play are always there. Even when we are not fully aware of it, playing plays a very important role in our lives—and we rarely give it up, really. You might not be playing in the school yard anymore, but from happy hour drinks to company team buildings and even how you spend your time on the internet, you are constantly drawn to games and having fun.

Because, and I circle back to what I was saying in the beginning, most people take humor lightly, but the vast majority of us have a constant, unconscious thirst for people who are light-hearted and fun. And this "vast majority of us" includes men, as much as women.

## WHAT BEING FUN ACTUALLY MEANS

OK, so being fun is really important for human beings, for one reason or another. It might be our brain seeking to get "high" on happy hormones or it might be our innate desire to be around people who make us forget about worries, stress, and anxiety.

Whatever it is, being fun is a social connector, at work, when dating, when spending time at home with our loved ones, or when meeting new people in different social contexts.

What does it actually mean to be fun, though?

Is it making jokes all the time?

Going on roller coasters every Saturday?

Being unpredictable and spontaneous?

Dancing on tables?

Well, being fun is a bit of all of that, minus the dramatic factor. Making jokes is fun, but you might not want to overdo it. Roller coasters are also fun, but when people predict you'll be on the next adrenaline-seeking endeavor every other week, you become a little more predictable in their eyes. Being unpredictable and spontaneous are also at the very foundation of being fun, but same as jokes, they should be balanced.

As for dancing on tables, well, that's up to you, really. If it's time to dance on a table then, girl, carpe diem.

Being fun is when you're a joy to be around, just like that. It is when you are the light-hearted breath of fresh air who loves to laugh and sees the full side of the glass all the time. It is when you're the kind of person people want to be around more than anyone else, the kind of person they call to take on adventures or attend their event because they know you'll always bring the "fun" touch everywhere you go.

Fun people are spontaneous in the sense that they're open to new experiences and ready to take new challenges from life. In general, men find a woman who is inflexible to be boring, so they will naturally lean towards ladies who are more spontaneous and, well, fun. These are the ladies who will go out on an impromptu date in the middle of the week (more on that later) and the ladies who don't need six months of planning in advance to go on a short trip out of town.

Being fun is being able to enjoy the little things, even when all the playbook rules say you shouldn't: an ice cream as big as your head every now and again and a night of drinking and dancing regardless of how old you may be.

Are you fun?

Well, think of it: do you see people calling you up to do something silly, or are they more likely to see you as "too serious for that"? Do you make people laugh? Are they excited to tell you funny stories because they know you're an easy laugh?

Men like women who are fun and laugh easily, precisely because it shows you have a good sense of humor and are open-minded. In consequence, this also makes them feel appreciated for their efforts to entertain you.

Research (Geher, 2013) has shown that both men and women appreciate a good sense of humor in their potential partners. However, while men define "having a good sense of humor" as "laughing at my jokes," women define the same term as "making me laugh." So men prefer women who laugh at their stories, while women prefer men with plenty of these stories.

Sounds equitable, right?

## WHAT IS NOT FUN?

Just like people don't take being fun as a serious matter, they also tend to be unnecessarily overzealous when it comes to the same quality. In other words, they overdo it—and not in the sense that they are super fun all the time, but in the sense that they take being fun to the extreme where it becomes bothersome (to say the least).

So, what is not fun?

Fun is not hurting anyone's feelings. The moment your being fun intercedes with someone else's emotions, it becomes something else entirely. To give you an example, bullies think of themselves as pretty fun when they hurt their victims, but the sad truth is that they are just scared kids who want to be in control.

Likewise, some women think it's fun (?) to control another person. Keep in mind that the man you are dating is an autonomous human being, just as you are —so no, there's nothing fun and definitely nothing healthy about trying to control them in any kind of way. This is not what irresistible women are made of.

Nagging and criticizing and constantly trying to change someone you're with are also forms of control —and no man (or woman!) should ever take this lightly. Quality men will simply not tolerate it, while average men will resent you for it.

In the end, both men and women want to be accepted for who they are in a relationship, and this is critical. If you like who you're dating and if you are with the right person, you will not want to change them. If you don't like who they are, then don't date them. It's as simple as that. Forcing anyone into something or someone you have pictured in your head will simply lead to heartache on both ends.

You can't sculpt the man of your dreams. You can only sculpt the "you" of your dreams who'll naturally attract the right match.

## BEING FUN AND BEING THOUGHTFUL

Being thoughtful is an essential element of being fun. Yes, making jokes and making people laugh (or easily laughing at what people have to say) is great.

At the end of the day though, nobody can be crazy fun all the time, and men are most likely not looking for someone who is just laughing every minute of every day. Beyond fun, men look for women who are thoughtful (just like women want a man who'll bring them flowers too).

A lot of times, being thoughtful is an underrated element or sub-branch of being fun. The light-heartedness that makes you laugh out loud at his jokes is the same warmth of spirit that makes you ask if they're OK when they have a tough day ahead.

It's also where all the fun little surprises that keep the connection alive come from:

- The little links you send him to make him smile
- How you let him know his favorite band is in town
- Offering to have some food delivered to their house when, after a few dates, you learn that they have a big, stressful day ahead of them

Grand gestures and names written in the skies?

Well, sure, yeah, they're fine. But they usually only happen in the movies and their recipients are usually women, not the other way around.

In real life, good men are just looking for ladies who will show them little acts of fun throughout the day, throughout the dinner dates, and, who knows, maybe throughout growing old together as well.

To put it in smarter words,

Research shows we don't really fall in love with a person — we fall in love with how we feel when we're with them. This is best demonstrated by the concept of emotional contagion: We're bad at telling what made us feel a certain way, but good about making associations. (Barker, 2014)

The best way to exemplify this is when you're doing a date recap with your friends and you can't remember exactly what he said but you definitely remember how he made you laugh all night.

## HOW TO BE MORE FUN

So far, we've established that:

- Being fun is great (what a surprise!)
- Being fun means being spontaneous, light-hearted, and open-minded
- Being fun also means being thoughtful and attentive with the little things
- Being fun does not mean being manipulative and controlling

But how do you make sure you are (or aren't) all these things?

How to be more fun?

Well, the thing with being fun is that there's no right or wrong way to do it (except when, as mentioned in the previous section, it hurts someone else). In essence, you make up your own definition of being fun, and your partner will have their own definition of the same term too.

For some, being fun means rock-climbing every weekend and partying until the sunrise.

For others, it might just mean video games and movies (probably also until the sunrise).

And for others, it might mean going to the theatre and taking pottery lessons together.

Your idea of fun might be wildly different than that of others, and that's perfectly fine. In fact, it is precisely one of the key ingredients that makes you unique and helps you attract like-minded people.

So, in this paradigm where "being fun" is defined in a thousand and one (or, better said, *seven billion*) ways, how do you level up?

While I cannot give you specific tips (because everyone defines their "fun" differently, remember?), I can give you some advice that will help you upgrade your fun, according to your definition.

### Invest In Your Relaxation

You can't be a fun person if all you do all the time is be anxious and stressed out. Yes, I know these are not buttons you can just switch off, but try to invest in your relaxation as much as you can.

Take some time off, do the things you love. Paint, run, or watch TV if that's what takes your mind off of day to day struggles. You need this. You deserve this.

### Feed Your Curiosities

Nurture and feed a genuine curiosity for life. Whether it is curiosity on how people in other countries eat or curiosities about history, science, how plants grow, or just how your favorite designers create their fashion pieces, nurture it.

Your curiosities make you interesting and fun.

### *Practice Being Around People*

And more importantly, practice being natural and open around them. It might not come easy if you are naturally introverted, but even so, you can definitely practice it. Keep in mind, this is not advice for you to change how you are, it is just advice to encourage you to get out there.

The more natural you are in the middle of people, the more fun people will perceive you to be.

### *Show Others You're Easy Going*

Show people you are not rigidly stuck within a set of rules (whether yours or socially established ones). Show them you like them: laugh at their jokes, maintain eye contact, keep the conversation alive with unique ideas, even if they sound crazy or unheard of.

Of course, only do this if it doesn't violate your moral boundaries. If that is the case, politely step away from the conversation and let it be. You do not owe anything to anyone if it correlates with something you do not believe in or something you are strongly against.

### Always Keep Your Mind Open

Open-mindedness is essential to being fun. Don't judge anyone, based on surface level information because you have never (and you will most likely never) walked a mile in their shoes with their baggage and their personality. This doesn't mean that it's okay to walk into dark alleys with strange men. If someone gives you a bad vibe you should probably trust that feeling. Please stay safe! But also stay curious about what makes people tick because it's fun and the world is full of wonderful and interesting people.

### Always Push Your Limits

People who push their limits are more likely to be in situations that make for great stories. Of course, this is not about pushing your limits in an unhealthy way (physically or psychologically), but about pushing them in a way that is controlled and productive.

Push your limits when rock climbing, when singing, when cooking, or just at work. Whatever you choose to do with your time, always strive to be better. And then even better—because personal growth is sexy.

### Don't Take Yourself So Seriously

People like those who aren't overly rigid. However, keep in mind that one tactic that's overused is self-deprecating humor. It's the staple of many stand-up comedians because it's funny but it's not without its insidious drawbacks.

Be wary of self-deprecating humor because our self-talk is more powerful than most people realize. Being able to laugh at things that didn't pan out the way you thought will make you more pleasant to others. At the same time, laughing at situations is great, while laughing at yourself as a person subtly undermines your value.

### *Find Your Sense of Humor*

Some people are more about situational humor, others are more about irony. Some people tell stories from their own lives, others tell the best jokes they found on the internet over breakfast.

They are different kinds of humor, and they are all amazing. Find yours and cultivate it—sooner or later, you will attract a man who matches up to your sense of humor.

### *Be Present in the Moment*

Enjoy the moment, seize the minute. People who constantly worry about the future tend to be perceived as less fun than others. Yes, you should plan for the future—but do make sure you don't lose the meaning of *today* in the process.

Live every second of your life in the present, with its ups and downs. Not only will this make you fun in other people's eyes, it will also be healthy for you. Living in the future can cause anxiety, living in the past can cause depression, living right now is perfection.

### *Leave Negativity Behind*

People do not like those who only see the empty half of the glass all the time. Nobody says you should be an incurable optimist, but leaving negativity behind and bringing a little bit of positivity into your mindset will eventually reflect in how you mirror yourself in the world. As a result, it will also make you more fun in the eyes of others.

Nobody can tell you what kind of fun you should be. That's up to you to decide. Once you do, however, feed this little fun child in you, for it will only bring you benefits (and not just for your dating life).

Being fun might be the tip of our irresistible woman iceberg, but it sure is a crucial part—so take it as seriously as possible! Tag, you're it!

Chapter Two

# FLIRTY

"Flirting is considered a universal and essential aspect of human interaction"

— T. JOEL WADE & ANDREA FELDMAN (WADE & FELDMAN, 2016).

It seems now that, ever since the dawn of mankind, people have always thought that only "young ones these days" flirt. The truth is quite different, though: in one form or another, flirting has always been there.

It might not have been as direct as it is today, but men and women have always sent each other sparks to show their interest in each other. It might have been smiles on social occasions (like balls and dances, for example). Or it might have just been talking at school or at work.

Whatever channel of flirty communication might have been socially acceptable at any given time in our history, there was always *something* that allowed people to show interest in each other.

Social expectations somewhat managed to distort the game of flirting at some point, when arranged marriages were the norm. But somehow, we always found our way back to primordial pre-mating playfulness.

To help you understand that flirting has always been part of our culture, let me talk a little about love and passion as Westerners perceive it. According to Denis de Rougemont, courtly love (or *amor courtois* in French) was a very serious game we borrowed from Arabic cultures via troubadours who visited Spain and the South of France first, and then spread the same courtly love traditions up North, to the nowaday territory of the United Kingdom (Rougement, 1995).

Courtly love was all about brave knights seeking adventure and fighting for the welfare of their *ladies*.

In appearance, that might sound like the foundation for pretty much every fairytale you have ever read or listened to. The reality of the courtly love tradition was a little more intricate, though.

The knight *did* seek to please the lady he professed his love by performing acts of bravery. What movies and modernly twisted stories don't tell you, however, is that their love was forbidden from the very beginning—the lady was already *given* to the King, the one whose vassal the knight was.

Their love was, thus, platonic. The knight kept professing his love to the lady to show not only his affection towards her, but also his loyalty towards his lord. The moment the love story between the knight and the lady became carnal in any way, they were doomed to suffering precisely because the passion between them was consummated.

The "play" between the knight and his lady went against natural instincts. You do not flirt or perform acts of bravery for someone you know you can never even touch—and yet, that was the ideal courtly love aspired to. In absence of pre-marriage flirting (because marriages were arranged and based on power and money, rather than love and passion), people sought different ways to fulfill their desire to flirt.

Going (or coming) back to modern days, the vast majority of people do not have to go through arranged marriages, except for those in a number of cultures where this is still common. These days, we choose our mates, and while this has given us plenty of freedom, it has also made things a lot more complicated.

Instead of letting our parents' thirst for keeping and multiplying fortunes and social authority decide our marital fate, we now do all this on our own. From the hundreds or maybe thousands of people of the opposite sex we meet throughout our lifetime, we are supposed to choose the one who will share our happiness and sadness in a way that is compatible with us.

Although steady relationships and marriage are very serious matters, flirting and playfulness still play a crucial role in bonding people together and setting them on the path to, well, long-lasting love (or any other kind of love you might be searching for, really).

We flirt not only because we like it (and oh, we do!). We flirt because it allows us to mate with someone suitable for us. In fact, flirting is so natural that you'll see it in other species in the animal kingdom too (such as male animals fighting for a mate or female animals picking the best of suitors based on given characteristics that denote power and good genes).

Of course, I am not comparing human relationships and flirting with animal foreplay. Men are obviously a lot more complex than waving pretty feathers for female attention, and human flirting is a game a lot more intricate than male baboons fighting to get the pretty she-baboon in a clan.

My point here is that there is nothing more natural than flirting. We have an intrinsic desire to mix play and finding a good mate in our genes—and as the superwoman you are, you should definitely tap into your power to do just that: flirt.

So, after this long (but hopefully revealing and interesting) prelude, how exactly do you flirt and where does being flirty lie in your way to being an irresistible woman?

Well, that's exactly what we'll talk about in this chapter.

## FLIRTING: THE LEVEL UP

If being fun is what opens you up to people (men included), flirting is your level up, the upgrade that will take you from the "nice girl next door" to "potential mate." And it's not just men who think this way, actually. Women too will perceive a man as a potential suitor when he shows interest in them (and that's exactly where flirting kicks in).

Your "being fun" was the tip of the iceberg, the magnet that brings people around you and helps you show the greatest parts of yourself. Your "being flirty" means moving to the next stage, where you interact with men you're interested with at a slightly deeper level.

Flirting is where your jokes turn into cute compliments and signs that you are paying attention to the guy you are talking to and seeing him as more than a friend. You can have fun with all the people in the world, but you are likely to only actually flirt with those you have at least a little bit of interest in.

What is fascinating about all this is that flirting is a two-ended game. You can't ignite it on your own. In fact, scientific research shows that people's expectations that the other person was going to like them was a major marker on the way to falling in love. This discovery was made by Dr. Arthur Aron, who, as a psychologist at the State University of New York, went as far as drawing thirty-six questions meant to make people come closer to each other in sixty minutes or less (Barker, 2014).

In Dr Aron's words (about how being liked influences whether we like someone or not), "If you ask people about their experience of falling in love, over 90 percent will say that a major factor was discovering that the other person liked them" (as cited in Barker, 2014).

So, in other words, flirting is how you take a connection with someone from "two people who have a good time together" to "romantic interest." If you or the other person never make that first leap, however, you will never know if romantic interest is even on the table. In fact, you'll never even put it on the menu—and in love affairs, almost nobody goes for the "secret menu items," jumping from "we're having a good time together" to the first date.

The courting ritual *needs* some sort of flirting as a bridge of connection between "fun" and "romantic." And no, flirting does not have anything to do with bouncy sorority girls squeezing a guy's muscles and saying "I like men with big muscles." That only works in two circumstances:

- Very young people who are not yet accustomed in the act of courtship, nor are they prepared for mature relationships
- In movies (sorry, but over the course of this book, you'll get some other hints of things that only actually happen behind the cinema screens)

Flirting doesn't mean asking the guy out either. You are free to take charge, of course, but if it comes out of the blue, the man you want to date might get a little defensive. The saying that "men make the first move" is both true and false.

On one hand, men make the first move traditionally because they are the ones courting the woman. On the other hand, most men would not even dare make the first actual move without getting hints that there's romantic interest between them and you.

So ultimately, the *very* first move (getting flirtatious) can happen on either end: yours or his. Do keep in mind that men and women define "flirting" in essentially different ways, and this is a fact proven by actual research (Wade & Feldman, 2016).

Women know that someone is flirting with them when that person shows signs of commitment (like asking them out, showing them attention, or listening to them). This comes from a very deep rooted desire all women have when seeking for a mate: knowing that they will be there and that the man's power will protect them and the family.

Sure, things have obviously changed in modern times and women don't necessarily stay at home to raise children and take care of the house, but at a DNA level, our deepest instincts lean towards how our primitive ancestors organized their society (*why* they did that exactly is a completely different discussion).

Men, on the other hand, tend to be a little more carnal, as they are likely to find a sexual mate in order to procreate. Their main deep instinct tells them that they have to spread their genes forward and have babies. As such, they will perceive physical interactions as flirting. In a study ran in 2016, men voted "having sex with him," "rubbing against him," and "dancing with him" as the most effective means of flirting (Wade & Feldman, 2016).

Alright, you might not want to just start rubbing against that cute friend of a friend you keep seeing in your social circle, or at least not completely all of a sudden. It takes a little to get there, and actions such as touching his arm, moving closer to him, making eye contact and actually listening to him are how you first level up from "almost strangers" to "people who might be dating in the (near) future."

More on how exactly to flirt, however, in the next section.

To take this first section to a conclusion, why should you flirt, specifically?

First of all, because it's in our nature and because it's part of the courtship process.

Secondly, because there are pragmatic reasons to do it. You don't want to actually take the lead in courtship and chase a man, but you want to playfully let them know you find them attractive. In doing so, you are also letting them know it's a good idea for them to chase you—and that's where things really take off.

Last, but definitely not least, flirting is fun, especially when you get good at it (and frankly, girl, that should be reason enough).

## HOW TO FLIRT

Despite what many people believe (men and women alike, by the way), flirting and rocket science have nothing in common—except, perhaps, the ignition of some sort of "fire" between different elements.

Flirting comes natural because it *is* natural. What might make you feel a little awkward about flirting (or, OK, downright anxious if that is the case) is not the act itself. It is the social conditioning and the negative self-talk wearing off on you.

All that "girls should be nice and always let the man make the first move" and all that "I'm not good at this"? Yep, those things are ruining your odds of meeting and dating men you actually want in your life.

Flirting is a really fun game when you get to learn the rules. It's like ping-pong, but instead of a little white ball, you use all your weapons, on both ends, to make passes at each other. You use your womanly weapons to show men you're interested, they use their weapons to show you they want to be with you. A tale as old as time!

I'll tell you two secrets now. Before I got into psychology and studying interpersonal relationships, I thought of myself as not that great with flirting. Frankly, I thought someone like me, who spent most of her time with her nose in books, would never be able to make advances to a man—and much less a man she had a crush on.

Boy, was I wrong! Flirting is a lot easier than I thought, and that's mostly related to how I changed my perception of myself. As I was saying earlier in the book, your self-talk can really influence how you project yourself into the world. Change how you talk to yourself and, slowly and steadily, you will change how you talk to others too (and yes, that includes the opposite sex as well).

The second secret I want to share with you is how I found my flirting rhythm. It's a little ridiculous, but whenever I started flirting with a man, I always played some sort of girl power 80s song in the back of my head. Two examples I can think of are Pat Benatar's *Love is a Battlefield* and Cyndi Lauper's *Girls Just Wanna Have Fun*. Cheesy, I know, but it worked because I learned that flirting is more like dancing than anything else—and those songs gave me the beat.

You might not like my song examples and I totally understand that (I mean, the 80s were *four decades ago*). But if you have a song you like and that makes you feel empowered, play it in the back of your head, in the background, while completely focusing on the person in front of you too. It can do wonders with social and dating anxiety, trust me!

And now, here are other tips you should consider when flirting:

- Keep it playful. This is flirting, not building rockets to land on Mars and not curing incurable diseases. If it works, it works; if it doesn't, then it's probably a funny story. If you keep your mindset on the positive side, you will attract the right man for you sooner rather than later.

So don't take yourself too seriously when flirting. We'll get to the more serious stuff later on in the book, and I definitely think those parts are extremely important. For now, though, just play the ball from your court to his and back. Feel the ground, dip your toes in the water, and most importantly, have fun!

- Keep it classy. As I said, being flirty has nothing to do with touching a guy's muscles and telling him he's hot. You can totally do it, but if you're looking to attract a man into your arms (and make him interested in staying there), that might not be the very best way to do it.

Flirting can and should be classy. It should be about the mind games more than the physical ones (because even if men are more physical in how they perceive flirting, the good ones will always prefer a lady).

- Don't be afraid of a little good spirited teasing. You might not want to do this with someone you don't know very well, but if you have already met each other and talked to each other, a little bit of teasing can make things more fun.
- Compliment him, but make sure you don't overdo it, as that might come across as needy. Toss in a little verbal appreciation about his charisma, sense of humor, hard work, or

talent—these are things any quality man would appreciate.

- Smile, and do it a lot. We're naturally more inclined to like people who smile at us, and men are no exception to this rule. Plus, smiling shows the guy you like spending time with him, and that's always a good sign.

- Ask them questions and actually listen. We all like being listened to, and, again, men are no exception from the norm. Listening to what they have to say makes them feel important and interesting and it shows them you genuinely want to spend time with them.

- Gently and playfully touch their arm or their shoulder or when you're ready to really escalate things, then touch his face. It's pretty amazing to see how much a human touch can account for, especially in situations like these! You don't want to overdo this, and you want to make sure you've been talking for long enough for you to break the space boundary (which, by the way, you can test by simply getting a little closer to them).

All in all, there's no recipe or transcript for the perfect "flirting session." Everyone is different and as such, the interactions between different people will also be, you guessed it, *different*. Play a little and give yourself some time to define your own flirting style. See what works for you and the men you want to attract and what doesn't. Test your flirting techniques on different men and see how they react.

Most importantly though, give yourself time to grow into this. Remember: it all starts in your brain. All the insecurities you might have in connection to flirting are nothing but a construct, something that's entirely made-up by your brain, your perceived experiences, and social expectation rules you should definitely ignore in the 21st century.

## HOW NOT TO FLIRT

OK, so we have established the ground rules on how to flirt. It might not be easy peasy lemon squeezy at first if you have not done this before, but like any skill, it's something you can learn, practice, and perfect.

To help you even further on this, here are some things you might want to avoid doing when flirting:

- Don't make your suitor feel bad in any way. There are literally hundreds of ways you might do this, and sometimes inadvertently. For example, you might be cruel with someone who wants to flirt with you, but you do not want to reciprocate their playfulness.

You might also want to be cruel with someone you are flirting with by igniting their jealousy or manipulating their thoughts and emotions. I cannot emphasize this enough: do not do it. Never, ever do anything manipulative to anyone (including, but not limited to the men you want to date or are dating). Yes, some dating coaches advise you to do this, but it is not fair towards the person you're flirting with. In fact, it is downright abusive.

Things like "There are a lot of cute guys at this party. Are you jealous?" should never be said. At the very least, they will just make the other person feel insecure. At the very worst, it will completely distance you from them (sooner or later).

- Don't make it all about you. Remember this for all your social interactions (be them romantic or not): people are a lot more interested in themselves than they are in you, especially when they do not know you very well.

That's not to say you should dedicate your time to anyone who makes it all about *them*. This is just to say that quality men will pass the ball in your court as an act of reciprocity and to show you their interest—and you should behave the same. Because yes, even when flirting, respect should still lie at the very foundation of the interaction between you and the other person. Otherwise, you're building a relationship on quicksand, and sooner or later, it's all going to crumble and fall.

No, flirting is not that hard. It takes a little to learn the ropes and learn what's OK and what isn't, but once you get into it, you'll never get out. And what's best, even once you are settled in a happy relationship, flirting and fun will always be there, together with all the deeper elements we will discuss in future chapters.

Being fun and being flirty are, indeed, just the surface. They are how you attract men and how you show them you're open to dating them. Over the next chapters, we will talk a little more about the fabric of building strong, honest, long-living and *happy* relationships.

# Chapter Three

# GENUINE

*"Be the same person privately, publicly, and personally"*

— JUDAH SMITH (SMITH, 2019)

D*oes any of this sound familiar?*

*"25 Ways to Trick Him Into Liking You"*

*"Get in His Head...and In His Bed"*

*"21 Sneaky Trick to Get Guys to Do What You Want"*

These are actual titles from women's magazines—headlines you have probably stumbled upon one too many times as well. Sure, things might have changed a little in the past ten years or so, and there's less "tricking" and more "realness" to how these magazines advise women.

Even so, it seems that, for decades, all we've ever been taught is to somehow lure men into our dens and pretend we're different from our real selves. And then, almost surprised, thousands and thousands of women and men woke up in relationships and marriages that made them feel nothing but terribly confused, asking themselves two essential questions that lead to marital/relationship issues:

- *Who am I and how do I get myself back?*
- *Who is this woman next to me and has she always been like this?*

Decades of personal and emotional mismanagement have made for generations of people who ended up living miserably next to someone who was not right for them.

In the wake of a time where honesty and being true to yourself matter more than anything, it is high time we changed the general perception on how women should behave "around men" too. And being genuine is just that: being authentic and allowing your real self to shine through.

Because, at the end of the day, you want to meet and date someone who likes you for who you are, not for whatever image of supposed perfection you're trying to project in the exterior.

Being genuine is the first element that goes beyond the surface of our Brilliant Vixen concept. If being fun and flirty are how you attract men in the first instance, being genuine (or authentic, as we will use the term interchangeably throughout this chapter) is how you start showing men there's more to you than "just" that.

## WHY ARE WE NOT NATURALLY GENUINE?

Regardless of what glossy magazines might advise these days, there seems to be a tendency for both men and women to behave somewhat unnatural when they're around the person they want to attract.

The "thing" with all these tricks that tell you to behave a certain way is that they can only work for a limited amount of time. You might "draw him in," but keeping him there and even more, being happy together, will most likely not be a matter of "tips and tricks" you get from outdated magazines or online articles.

As a side note, I just want to emphasize the fact that I am not dismissing any kind of magazine, article, or author. In fact, you should definitely read as much as possible, from as many sources as possible.

What you should also do, however, is learn how to filter the information you get through your own perspective, personality, goals, and personal history. It doesn't matter if something "magically" worked out on someone else out there—if it doesn't feel right for you in your heart and mind then you won't stick with it.

To circle back to the topic of this chapter, being insincere (with yourself and the other person) is the shortest path you can take to heartache (on our end, as well as theirs). And yet, so many people still do it.

Why so? Why are we so inclined to not show our true selves, not even to those who are supposed to become our partners?

Well, there are a few primary reasons:

### *We Are Taught to Be Ladies*

I am not, in any way, shape, or form, dismissing the idea of being ladylike. Nor am I dismissing the idea of behaving womanly.

However, those are things you should do not because society dictates it, but because it's how you actually are. If cooking and wearing dresses are just not your thing, then nobody should try to force you into doing that just for the sake of attracting men.

As little girls, we're taught to behave within very specific parameters. Boys are raised with their own set of expectations, but girls tend to be more pushed in a traditional gender role-based paradigm.

- Sit like this, not like that
- Little ladies should not speak out like that
- A woman should...
- A woman shouldn't...
- You'll never find Prince Charming if you keep your hair/clothes/walk like that
- These aren't games for little girls
- Those movies/games/toys are for boys!

From a very young age, "little ladies" are conditioned to conform to certain stereotypes. I am, of course, generalizing, and I am fully aware that the way we raise our children has changed a lot in the past few decades—but as a woman in your 20s, 30s, or 40s, you might still have experienced at least remnants of that kind of education.

And while you might not be fully conscious of this, all these conditions (on how a girl should or shouldn't be/say/play) have probably left a mark on how you treat your authenticity.

I'm not saying this is 100% the case for everyone. But even so, analyzing where you stand on this matter might help you not only rediscover your true self, but also let her free to enjoy the spotlight.

Because you know what?

A girl should only do one thing: be herself.

### *We Think Society Will Judge*

Whether we admit it or not, we all have our quirks and oddities. We all have those parts of ourselves that are not entirely up to par with societal expectations. We are all imperfect according to the highest standards of whatever society wants from us.

By showing their true selves, many people feel they are making themselves vulnerable in the eyes of the almighty societal scrutiny. We think we'll be judged if we don't fit a certain size and admit to it. We think we'll be judged if we do not behave a certain way or build a certain kind of life. We think we'll be judged if we do not fit the mold and run with the crowd.

The issue here is that this is all in your mind. In a world where plus-sizes are making the runways for the biggest designers on the globe and where we are all finally speaking up about stringent issues in women's lives, you can be anything.

Now, more than ever, society will not judge you. Au contraire, my dear reader: society will think of you as a hero and a warrior for accepting yourself and attempting to project your true self out into the world.

We live in an era where social and religious opression, as well as discrimination on a variety of grounds are being slowly (and steadily) won over. It might not happen everywhere in the world, sadly, and it might not be uniform even from one state to another.

But change is happening. And the more people choose to live authentically, the better off everyone will be in the end.

That being said there will always be critics, trolls, and haters but they will judge you no matter what you do so there's no point in living your life to try to please everyone if you want to be happy.

Here are some great quotes from some incredible people who would have never realized their dreams if they based their lives on other people's approval:

This quote is often misattributed to Aristotle, but is actually by writer Elbert Hubbard, from his book "John North Willys": "Do nothing, say nothing, and be nothing, and you'll never be criticized."

"You can be the ripest, juiciest peach in the world, and there's still going to be somebody who hates peaches." - Dita Von Teese

### *We Think We Will Not Be Accepted and Liked*

Another major reason we sometimes fail to be our true selves is because we think we will not be accepted and liked by those in our close proximity—like the person we're dating, for example.

We tell little white lies about how we like their new shirts, when, in fact, we don't. We say we like things we never even did (like football or a certain band or a movie). We find ourselves dismissing the things we do like just to make ourselves more pleasant in the eyes of others. And before we know it, we lose ourselves, our beliefs, and our life principles in a (desperate) effort to be liked.

What you need to know is that sooner or later, all this will just turn against you. You can "fake it 'till you make it" with a lot of things, but not with the things that matter to us (regardless of how you define what matters to you: your favorite band, your relationship with your family, or spiritual beliefs, for example).

Be the best version of yourself and you will attract someone who loves the **ultra you**!

## WHAT IS BEING GENUINE, EVEN?

After so many "do's" and "don'ts" (which, by the way, have changed over the course of the millennia), it seems that we have even lost the meaning of "being genuine."

According to the Macmillan dictionary, being genuine means being "real, rather than pretended or false." (Macmillan, 2020).

That is, of course, a very good definition, but it does not really encompass authenticity as we are discussing it in this chapter. Rather than just being "real" and "non-false," being genuine or authentic is about connecting with your innermost being and allowing that part of your own self to roam free into the world.

Sounds a bit too poetic, but here are some examples of what being genuine means:

- Genuine people are not always the most popular people, because they do not always say the nicest things (even if they do say it in a nice, empathetic way)

- Genuine people speak in accordance to their truth (which may or may not coincide with the truth of the world)
- Genuine people are sad sometimes (and show their sadness, to some extent at least) when they feel like it. They also laugh wholeheartedly when they feel like that.
- Genuine people don't say "I'm OK" when they aren't, nor do they fake some sort of issues in their lives just to get at the center of drama.
- Genuine people do not speak of others behind their backs, because they wouldn't like someone else to do this to them.
- Genuine people are polite, but that doesn't mean they always say "yes." In fact, they have learned to say "no" and they don't have to emit excuses for this.
- Genuine people stand by what they believe and like, even if it's an unpopular opinion, and even when it might mean their date will see them differently.

All in all, genuine people act from a place that values their own integrity. Their authenticity might not look the same as someone else's, and it might feel very real to some and very unreal to others. As long as **you** know what's real to you and you show it to the world, however, you're doing this whole "being genuine" thing right.

Being authentic and genuine is not only healthy for how you date, but also for you, as a person. Humanistic psychologists tout the benefits of authenticity, psychopathologists underscore the impact a lack of authenticity has on the self, and all in all, researchers show that being true to your own self actually makes you happier (Hopper, 2018).

Even if you leave the whole dating scene aside, being happier by being closer to yourself is an offer you can't refuse.

All in all, the core concept of being genuine is not necessarily flexible. However, the way in which **you** express it is the epitome of "open to interpretation." Being genuine is about showing who you are as an individual. It's about showing who you *really* are without reservation or fear of judgment—simply because you know the best way to live is a life where you allow yourself to not talk yourself out of what you truly believe in.

## WHAT IS NOT BEING GENUINE?

Alright, so we have established what being genuine means (at least in broad terms).

What does it not mean, then?

Well, being genuine has nothing to do with being blunt, rude, or downright mean. Someone who's genuine is not:

- Someone who "tells it like it is"
- Someone who "keeps it real"
- Someone who "has no filter"
- Someone who is "just being honest"

In some ways, being authentic includes all of the above, but summing up the entire definition of being genuine to any of the aforementioned bullet points would add a negative connotation to it—and that's definitely not correct.

Yes, genuine people tell it like it is and keep it real, but in a way that is kind and compassionate, not snarky and mean. Yes, genuine people are always honest because living truthfully means telling the truth. But no, genuine people are not just "filterless," they do not just spit out everything they want to say, any way they want to say it.

Being mean and cruel and letting yourself off the hook with a flippant "I'm just being honest" is not what authenticity is all about. Not even in the slightest.

Mind you, there's a pretty thin balance between being genuine and slipping into being *too* open. Psychologists speak about self-monitoring, the ability to adapt your behavior according to your environment. They say that too much self-monitoring will disconnect you from your true self by enabling inauthenticity (and thus, unhappiness). At the same time, someone who's not self-monitoring enough will be unhappy because they will have difficulties behaving appropriately for the environment.

Finding the right balance will make you a happier person in the end (within and outside the dating spectrum). After all do you really want to be the kind of person who sees something genuinely funny and lets out peals of loud laughter...at a funeral?

## WAYS TO BE MORE GENUINE

We have defined being genuine and we have discussed not being genuine; but what about how to be more genuine, more authentic to your true self? What are the specific ways to *get there*?

The bad news is that nobody can give you a recipe here, and even more so since authenticity and discovering one's authenticity is a very personal and individualistic process. As such, what worked for someone else might not work for you and it might just end up conditioning you in someone else's full definition of "being genuine."

The good news is that there are a few things you can do to cultivate your own authenticity:

- Redefine vulnerability. You should only be very vulnerable in front of a very few select people, not everyone (and yes, "everyone" here includes someone you've just started out dating too). However, to make sure you do not hide your true self, you should also redefine how you understand "being vulnerable." There's nothing wrong about showing sadness when that's how you feel, for example, but you might not want to share the actual reason or extent of your sadness with everyone either.
- Learn how to be present. Mindfulness exercises (whether yoga or reading or any other similar type of practice) can definitely help you here. The more present you are, the more connected you are with your inner self,

every moment of every day. Being present allows you to stop and recalibrate yourself in different life situations and environments according to your own beliefs and true personality.

- If showing the genuine you is an intimidating idea then perhaps start small, with spaces and people that make you feel safe, and work your way up from there. Another counterintuitive strategy is to be completely yourself with total strangers who you don't expect to see again. The stranger strategy works because you have absolutely nothing to lose in those short-term relationships so the pressure is far less.

- Being in an environment that supports your true self 100% is fantastic. Let's say you've always wanted to become a poet but you're afraid of being judged by your colleagues. Go to an open mic poetry night and talk to some other poets. Like attracts like, and being around what you love gives your heart permission to love it. If it isn't hurting you or anyone else why shouldn't you embrace it? If you need to start small that's okay! Moving forward no matter how slowly is still progress! Just know that the more you grab hold of this "true self" version of you, the more of it you will show to the world.

- Recognize your masks. You might not always be able to take them off entirely, but being aware of them will at least help you connect your true self to the reality of your moment. We all wear masks to some extent, but being aware of them makes the difference.

- Accept feedback. Good or bad, constructive or not, feedback is a gift. Take it as it is, learn from it, filter it through your own goals, perspectives, and personality, and take the most precious lessons with you.

Leave the filters at the door, but make sure you know when to shift the perspective of what you're saying so that it doesn't hurt someone else. For instance, if your best friend comes out of the changing room wearing a dress that just doesn't suit her, you can always tell her "let's search for something better," rather than "that's plain ugly" or "oh, my, that looks great on you!"

## EXAMPLES THAT DEMONSTRATE GENUINE BEHAVIOR

A genuine behavior can be translated in a lot of ways, so it would be impossible for a book (not to mention a chapter!) to comprise all the possible scenarios.

To give you an idea of what "being genuine" means in the Brilliant Vixen context, however, here are some examples:

**The Movie Talk**

"He: Hey, have you seen the latest Aquaman movie? I thought it was absolutely horrible!"

"You: Wow, really? Haha! I liked it, and I thought Jason Momoa somehow managed to make Aquaman cool (which, let's face it, is kind of difficult, right?)"

**The Football Game**

"He: Hey, wanna come with me to the game on Saturday?"

"You: Hmm... not sure if I'd be a very good company there, given I don't know much about football and frankly, it never caught on for me. Maybe meet you afterwards for drinks, what do you think?"

**The Political Debate**

"He: So, I'm kind of curious, who are you going to vote for this fall?"

"You: Well, I am not a very big fan of politics on dates, but I am very interested in finding out something else about you. Like, for example, what was your biggest hobby as a kid?"

## The Gossip

"He: Oh my God, that dude John, your workmate, is such a ladies' man!"

"You: Haha, really? I never really noticed and to be honest, I didn't quite care to look any closer. Speaking of ladies' men, what do you think of the new Aquaman movie?"

The list of examples can go on and on. There's no secret recipe to doing this right—just be true to what you like and believe and turn uncomfortable talks with a positive vibe. Don't accept agreeing to something just because it would be what your date is expecting. After all, this is dating: if it's meant to be and you two click, you will click regardless of who likes Aquaman or not.

Courtship is a time of maximum discovery, so allow your date to discover the **real you**, not what you think they want to discover in you. Sooner or later, the "fake you" will fade out and your partner will realize this as much as you will. It's better to be honest upfront and show the real self. It is the most honest, the healthiest, and the single most beneficial thing you can do for your future happiness.

# Chapter Four

# HIGH-VALUE

"Quality is not an act, it is a habit."

— ARISTOTLE (N.D.)

Birds of a feather flock together—and whether we like it or not, the statement applies in dating as well. You attract what you are and what you think you deserve (even if at an unconscious level).

Most women (and, in fact, most human beings) understand this at a basic level. They understand that what you are mirrors in who you are with, both when it comes to love relationships and when it comes to friendships, workplace, and so on.

If you believe you are unworthy, deep down, you will always settle for relationships that do not make you happy. If, however, you believe your time, energy, and love are worth a lot more, you will always search for someone who can offer you nothing less than what you want.

Careful though, that does not mean you can just ask people for everything and give nothing in return. A high-value woman does not just ask to never give anything—a high-value woman only "functions" on win-win, in love relationships and otherwise.

Being fun attracts, being flirty shows you're available, and being genuine shows you're more than that.

Being high-value is when a man can realize they are not just dating anyone, but the woman with whom he can rule the world in any way the two of you decide to do it. In this chapter, we will discuss more about what being high-value actually means, how to achieve it, and what it does *not* mean to be high-value.

Let's roll!

## WHAT IS A HIGH-VALUE WOMAN?

A high-value woman is a woman who not only knows her value, but also:

- Knows how to project it on the outside in a healthy, empowered, and feminine way
- Attracts men who respect her for what she is and who mirror her behavior on their end

Being high-value is the foundation upon which everything else in your future relationships with men will ever be built on.

It would be impossible to encompass everything a high-value woman is in a simple definition, but if we have to narrow it down, a high-value woman is the woman high-value men want to be with and the woman who will settle for nothing less than what she truly wants (in dating, as much as everything else in life).

High-value women continuously work on themselves to become their best versions. They do not settle—not for men who don't make them happy, and not for lesser versions of their own selves.

These women feel very grounded and unwavering when you are around them, and yet they manage to do this without being rough around the edges. When you are with a high-value woman, you unconsciously feel that you **need** to take her seriously because her time is valuable.

High-value women have magnetic personalities and they are also great communicators. They are very certain of who they are as people and they have a very well-defined sense of what's important to them.

In other words, high-value women have their sh**t together. They enjoy life, they live it on their own terms, and they are looking for someone who is just like them.

In this section of the fourth chapter, we will move through the high-level pillars of what high-value women are. In the following sections, we will explain some of the most common characteristics high-value women possess, as well as explore a little deeper the characteristics which these women do not possess.

### *High-Value Women Do Not Complain about the Mundane*

Complaining about every little bad thing that happens throughout your day is not even about being nagging.

It is about communicating a message that doesn't do you justice.

When you complain about something minor, that doesn't have any kind of value (not even truly negative), you are communicating about things that do not matter (not even to you, really). You are just sending out bad vibes for things you do not actually care about.

This kind of low-vibrational communication does nothing but kill the mood—and eventually kill romance.

Here are five examples of communications between a man and a woman. Look at them, read them closely, and decide which ones involve a high-value woman or not (based on everything you have learned about being a high-value woman so far in this chapter).

**Example #1**

Him: *How was your day?*

Her: *It sucked! I was stuck in traffic for 3 hours today, then when I went to the post office they tried to close 5 minutes early but I demanded that they take my package.*

**Example #2**

Him: *How was your day?*

Her: *Not too bad, it actually reminded me of a TED talk I saw regarding time being flexible...have you ever felt that way?*

**Example #3**

Him: *How was your day?*

Her: *I can't complain. I just remembered that I read an article this morning that made me think of you.*

Him: *Oh yeah what was it?*

Her: *Did you see that there was a new type of dinosaur discovered in Mainland China today? It was a medium sized carnivore from the late Cretaceous period.*

Him: *That's amazing! NO I didn't see that at all. Do you remember the name? I want to check it out.*

(As a side note, if you think that this reaction is over the top you are clearly underestimating the number of guys who still love dinosaurs just as much as when they were kids! Their kid-like enthusiasm can be pretty endearing and bonding over childhood loves can create a new level of closeness.)

## Example #4

Him: *How was your day?*

Her: *Not bad. I'm really excited about this new art project I'm working on.*

Him: *A new art project, cool what is it?*

Her: *I decided to try painting a picture of my mom's childhood dog. It's coming along really well but I only have 3 more days before her birthday.*

Him: *That's so thoughtful, good luck! You'll have to send me a picture when you're ready.*

## Example #5

Him: *How was your day?*

Her: *I'm not going to lie, today was rough but I believe that adversity is the state in which people get to grow the most. I've been reading some great stories from famous entrepreneurs who creatively overcame obstacles. It was really inspiring.*

Him: *Oh no, what happened?*

Her: *Nothing interesting but I did have to come up with a creative strategy for tomorrow that I think is going to yield great results.*

Him: *Best of luck to you. Either way, I'd love to take you out to dinner on Friday to either celebrate or recharge.*

Her: *Sounds perfect.*

As you have probably noticed, all of these examples can come from the same woman, on the same day. The difference lies in what the woman in these texts decides to focus on and what they decide to show to their love interest.

Imagine your day like a handkerchief. If it falls flat on the floor, you can pinch it to pick it up from any point. It will not look even if you pinch the outer sides, for example, but you can still pick it up—and regardless of which way you choose to do it, the handkerchief will be back in your hands (and off the ground).

If, however, you decide to leave it low, on the floor, that's exactly where it will be one hour from now. Even more, someone may accidentally step on it as well. Ugh!

If your conversation is like the handkerchief in this metaphor, you want to pick it up. You want to somehow pinch your conversation from any of the points that lay flat on the floor and get it off of there, back in your control. If you are too low to pick the discussion up and take it into a more positive direction, it will stay low and get dirty (and not in a good way).

Example #1 is the most mundane type of complaining you can do. Yes, we're all human and yes, we all do it sometimes. Doing it with someone you're dating, however, might make you seem boring, uninteresting, and superficial. Nobody wants to hear about being stuck in traffic, for example, because it happens to all of us (there's no worldwide conspiracy to only get *you* stuck in traffic).

In all the other examples, the man in the conversation is not leading with anything exciting. It is the woman who picks up the discussion and takes it into an area that might be of interest to the guy (such as a TED talk, dinosaurs, or simply using the moment to show you love a good challenge at work).

Apply these conversations to any real-life scenario and you will clearly visualize which of these versions actually "caught" the man and which one will be perceived as annoying, nagging, and complaining about things that do not really pose an interest to anyone.

### *High-Value Women Do Not Believe in Scarcity*

Low-value women settle, and there are many surface reasons they do that, but the underlying reasoning behind settling for less is always rooted in fear and scarcity issues. "There are no other men out there" and "This is good enough for me" are lies they keep telling themselves to rationalize the decision to stay with someone who is not making them happy.

There are several consequences to believing in the concept of scarcity (especially in dating, but the same consequences can be applied to any other area of one's life):

- You make hasty decisions

- You have weak or no boundaries at all
- You proceed further with something (or someone) even though your gut tells you something isn't right
- You leave yourself open to all kinds of mistreatments
- You operate out of the underlying fear that you do not want to be alone

I am not denying that there are even deeper reasons these fears and behaviors might be ruling your life. You might have been abandoned in the past by someone you loved (a parent). You might have been hurt. You might have low self-confidence that stems from a traumatic event.

Whatever it is, I want you to know this: **you can move on**. And it will be the best thing you will ever do for yourself.

Leaving the concept of scarcity behind is the ultimate secret to successful dating. If you want to share just one tip from this book with someone else (a friend, your family, etc.), may it be this: **there's no such thing as scarcity, there is enough to go around for everyone.**

When you leave scarcity behind, you automatically turn everything in your favor:

- You start thinking things through and ask yourself: *does this really work for me or not?*
- You have strong, non-negotiable boundaries
- You always trust your gut
- You don't tolerate any type of mistreatment

Let me try to explain scarcity with a real-life, non-dating example.

You are making an exquisite dessert for a special event, and just when you are almost through with everything, you realize you need some strawberries to top off your dessert. Obviously, you forgot to buy them last time you went to the grocery store, so you storm out of your house and run to the closest store.

There, you see there's only one box of strawberries left and they look quite bad. They are damaged and squished, they are not ripe, they lack color, and you have a sense that they lack taste as well. Not that great for the dessert you've worked so hard on, right?

You ignore all these bad characteristics and you snatch the box because, after all, it's the last one in the store and you need it right? So it will be just *good enough*.

Except they aren't. You're using them to top off your super-intricate dessert, the one you've been working on all day long. They're supposed to be the crowning jewel of your hard work and look at them: they are not even *close* to what you had in mind.

Wait a second, though! There are plenty of other grocery stores around you and you do not have to tolerate these miscreant berries, so why buy them then? You climb up to the produce section, holding the berries over your head, and yell: *"These are not the strawberries I was looking for and I refuse to settle for less than I deserve! Do you hear me, grocery store? All ladies, scream with me: free yourselves from the slow death called 'second best' and join me in a revolution for all womankind!"*

And just when you're at the top of your revolution, you feel someone tapping your leg and saying *"Excuse me, miss."* You look down and see a handsome store manager. *"We have just received some lovely organic strawberries, we're unloading them now. I'd be more than happy to grab you one if you like?"* he says smiling at you.

You unceremoniously drop the bad berries by your side and reply to him in a less frantic tone: *"Yes, that would be lovely, thank you!"* as you climb down from your makeshift mountain of produce.

Hey, why not shoot the cute manager a smile as if to say, *"I'll take your number as well because you were kind and thoughtful and you do not have a wedding ring on."*

To this, he replies by asking you if you'd be interested in running off to the South of France with him because he's not the grocery store clerk at all, but the owner of the whole chain...

OK, OK, I might have gone a little off-topic here. The main point is that scarcity is not real most of the time, and it is most definitely not real when it comes to dating. There's plenty to go around and you have a lot more romance options that are wonderful for you if you avoid the tunnel vision.

As a high-value woman, you believe there is enough success for everyone. As such, you will not settle for something less than what you always wanted.

### High-Value Women Know How to Handle Their Emotional Baggage

You know how, in the movies, over-complicated women with lots of emotional baggage always have an aura of mystery around them and they seem to always attract the best men in the entire cast?

Well yeah, that's in the movies.

In real-life, nobody wants to carry your emotional baggage, and especially when you don't want to deal with it yourself. You need to take responsibility for your choices and for your future.

Whatever defines your past, it's a bygone. It's in past tense. It happened. It might have been your mistake or someone who wronged you. But it stays in a timeline you cannot reach anymore. All you can do is grab your lessons and move forward keeping your head up high and your emotional baggage in check.

To put it in the words of a guy who changed how we view the human brain, Carl Jung, one of the parents of Psychology and Psychoanalysis: "I am not what happened to me, I am what I choose to become" ("A Quote by C. G. Jung," n.d.-a).

To put it all in a nutshell, high-value women stand up for something, and that polarizes men around them. You cannot fake being high-value. You must actually value yourself before anyone else will.

And when you do value yourself, you will be set apart from the pack. You will **command** not **demand** respect. Quality men will speak up and approach you with their best foot forward precisely because they know they will regret it if a woman of this caliber just passes them by.

As for the rest of men, they'll either just keep quiet or yell out something not expecting an actual reaction. If they were honest, they'd yell out *"I am not good enough to have anything to offer a woman like you and it's super depressing!"* But then again, if they had the mental clarity to do that in the first place, you wouldn't be in the position where they are catcalling you from a moving vehicle, would you?

## THE HIGH-VALUE WOMAN CHARACTERISTICS

Alright, so we have established a high-value woman:

- Does not complain and even avoids discussions about the mundane
- Does not believe in scarcity
- Knows how to handle her own emotional baggage and expects to be with someone who also has their emotions well sorted.

What else is there to a high-value woman?

Well, a lot. High-value women (and, in general, irresistible women) are complex and multi-layered in a way that doesn't make men want to pack their bags and flee to another country, but in a way that magnetizes the good men and keeps them close.

Here are some further qualities high-value women tend to possess:

- They are feminine. Keep in mind that femininity has little to do with actual attractiveness (as it is defined by the beauty

norms of any century or millennium).
Femininity is a way of being, breathing,
walking, and blinking. It's Audrey Hepburn
in a black dress looking at a storefront with
jewelry and Aretha Franklin as she
commands RESPECT on stage. Feminine
women carry themselves well, with poise and
elegance, even when they're wearing the
simplest T-shirt and pair of jeans outfit in
their wardrobe.

- They take good care of themselves. Again,
  this has nothing to do with weight, height, or
  size. It has to do with how you take care of
  your body (so that it takes care of you).
  Maintaining good hygiene, putting on a little
  bit of makeup, healthy hair that looks good,
  exercising because it makes you feel excellent
  —these are things all women can do
  regardless of how they meet or don't meet
  "traditional" beauty standards.

- They are emotionally intelligent. They know
  how to sense other people's emotions and
  fine-tune themselves accordingly. They know
  the right words, the right gestures, the right
  actions that actually help. High-value women
  genuinely care about people—both the ones
  they are dating and the world as a whole.

- They are excellent communicators. They do

not need to yell to convey a message in an assertive way, and this stems from their self-confidence, as much as their ability to "read" the room.

- They have strong boundaries. A high-value woman will not do something that goes against her values, beliefs, or wishes. Never, ever, not in a million years.
- They waste no time. They don't have time for nonsense and half-hearted behaviors. They will not give you a second chance and then a third one just to be disappointed. They know the red flags and they do not want to waste their time with people who do not value their true worth.
- They do not lie. It is underneath their value, their sense of self-worth and self-confidence. They expect absolute sincerity in everything and they are more than ready to offer the same.
- They are not about the appearance only. High-value women do take care of how they look, but this never comes at the cost of substance. They are beautiful inside and out, beyond current standards at any point in history, beyond age, beyond fashion trends.
- They are positive. High-value women do not feel the need to enforce their power through

anger or negativity. They know their strength can inspire people more than angry rants and screams.

- They always want to grow. They want to be better today than they were yesterday, in their career, at home, as people, as friends, and as lovers. They are actively working towards their goals, whatever area they might be in.

In essence, there are two main types of high-value women:

- The ones who are open and warm and welcoming to everyone but still maintain healthy personal boundaries
- The ones who are less approachable and only open up in front of a select few

Both are OK. However, keep in mind that taking the second approach has to be handled with care. If you tip the balance off just a little on the side of negativity, you might be perceived as more than just unapproachable, but as conceited and "just an image without the actual contents."

High-value women strike the perfect balance between strong and feminine, sweet and assertive, timeless and yet fashionable, smart yet not arrogant, emotionally intelligent yet not overly emotional. They are goddesses who know that while mainstream media chants about how men rule the world, the real rulers of the planet are (and have always been) Brilliant Vixenes. From the background or right in the limelight, high-value women have always shaped the world, civilization, culture, arts, and even politics.

Don't believe it? Open up a history book. There was always a woman who either raised or supported the man who was in charge. And there was always a woman who was herself a leader.

## WHAT A HIGH-VALUE WOMAN IS NOT

We have learned what high-value women are and the qualities they possess. What about misconceptions, then? What are the things high-value women are *not*, in any way?

I will keep this short:

- They are not always career women. It doesn't matter if you want to focus on your career, building a family, or both. You can be a high-value woman in any situation and you will excel at whatever you enterprise. Likewise, someone can be a low-value woman regardless of whether they focus on their careers or their families.

- They are not always the most educated, well-learned, or cultured. Yes, a high-value woman should know how to maintain the conversation and take it in a positive direction. However, that does not always mean reciting Shakespeare, discussing Kant philosophy, or discussing the latest approach in developing computer CPUs. If these are topics of interest to you, then sure. But don't feel like only a highly educated woman can be a high-value woman. It's not about that in any way.

- They do not necessarily come from the best families. You can come from any kind of family and still be a high-value woman. It's all about perfecting yourself, not being born with a perfect background.

- They do not always have a high IQ. If you do, congratulations. If you don't, learn that EQ (emotional intelligence quotient) is actually more important in how you are perceived by human beings and how successful you are in your endeavors (whatever they might be). Like it or not, humans are social animals, and a high EQ will actually help you navigate society and get to the top in whatever way you choose to define "success."

High-value women not only know what they want. They know how to go and get it because they know their power lies in their fight against mediocrity in every sense there is.

High-value women are leaders and followers, mothers and inventors, physicians and personal trainers, doctors and emotional support for their family and friends. They are simply **amazing**.

*Chapter Five*

# CHALLENGE

"The bigger the challenge, the bigger the opportunity"

— ANONYMOUS

Love may not be a battlefield in the sense Pat Benatar sang about in the 1980s, but it sure is a game. Mind you, as emphasized in previous chapters, playing "games" should never, *ever* involve hurting the one you're dating.

Posing some sort of challenge to the one you're dating will deepen their attraction towards you and make them see you as a suitable companion long-term. At the same time, it is highly important to make sure you know how to be a challenge, what areas to tap into, and when to stop being a challenge and start being warm and approachable.

There is a very big difference between being playful with someone and playing manipulative games with someone's emotions. These are not the "games" we're talking about. Striking the right balance here is essential to any healthy relationship, as you will learn in this chapter.

In short, what we will discuss here is *why* being a challenge is important, why it is crucial to calibrate this correctly, and how to be a challenge without being perceived as a threat to your date's self-confidence and lifestyle.

Without further ado, let's dive deeper into this topic!

## WHY YOU NEED TO BE A CHALLENGE

Just like with flirting, males will always like a female who poses a challenge. You see it everywhere in nature, where males fight for the one they want to mate with. Obviously, things are different when it comes to human "mating," but the instinct is still there: males want to fight for their females. They might not want to fist fight the guy at the bar who's trying to hit on you while you're on a date with them, but they will still want some sort of challenge.

One way or another, you have definitely encountered dating advice that sets you in this direction. Not being always available for a person, not calling him first after a date, not replying to text messages right away—these are things your friends, your mom, and some glossy magazines have surely recommended before.

While all the advice out there might be very wrong a lot of times, there are some gems here if done correctly. "Catch me if you can" is, in fact, the best attitude you can assume if you want not only to attract a man worth your time, but also make him want to ask you out on a second, third, and twentieth date.

There's nothing wrong with that. In the end, that's exactly how you are too. You are probably not very attracted to the nice guy next door who is always available for you and who poses zero challenge. With this guy, there are literally no fun games, and romance is killed quickly when he starts to mirror everything he thinks you want him to be: the guy who carries your purse and your luggage, the guy who will always say "yes" to whatever you want and say, the guy is just universally undesirable precisely because he makes himself look too soft, too sweet, and just too... not your type.

Posing a challenge is important not just because common knowledge dictates it, but because science dictates it as well. According to a research paper published in 2015 (Park et al.), men are actually attracted to someone who is their "level up" (in intelligence or fitness, for example).

This is also when things get complicated, because what do you know, *humans* themselves are pretty complex beings!

According to the aforementioned research paper (citing six other studies), men *do* say they are a lot more likely to want to be with someone who is more intelligent, fitter, or just better than they are in particular areas. In fact, a staggering 86% of men reported they'd be happy dating someone smarter than them.

Experiments showed, however, that this only happens when that woman (or dating her) is a psychologically distant event. This means that, once they'd get closer, men would feel intimidated or put down by a woman who is visibly boasting her better capabilities.

As defined by Sergiu Baltatescu (2014), "Psychological distance is a cognitive separation between the self and other instances such as persons, events, or times." Furthermore, psychological distance can be defined by different dimensions: spatial (which includes time as well), social, and hypothetical. When someone is psychologically distant from an event or space, they will describe it in more abstract terms, whereas when they are psychologically close, they will describe it in terms that are more concrete.

For instance, let's take Jack and Jill. Jack was told by a friend of his that Jill would make for a great match because she is a very fit lady and that would motivate Jack to go to the gym more often. From a psychologically distant point (in space and time), Jack is more than happy with the idea.

However, when he meets Jill for the first time and takes her bowling, she proves that her fitness and sporting capabilities are a lot higher than his. She wins the game by a large difference, which makes Jack feel inadequate, especially when compared to his own mental and social construct of how a man should be

His experience with Jill is, thus, negative, so he decides to not call her for a second date.

You see, the issue between Jack and Jill is not one of challenges. Jill did pose a challenge to Jack; however, her presentation of that challenge was not one that made Jack feel motivated, but the exact opposite. If she kept it fun and still flirted with him it could have worked out great.

For example, if you find something else to compliment him on but still enjoy playful teasing, that could still work. If he's super smart then you could say, "If bowling pins attack earth I got this but I still need you to be my Jeff Goldblum in *Independence Day* and infect the alien mothership with a virus, if I try to do it it'll just tell me I need to update Windows again."

If you've kept it fun and flirty and he's still pouty then it's probably not a good match. A sense of humor is important.

Used correctly, *challenge* can turn things the other way around. It could have stimulated Jack, for example—not only to call Jill for a second date, but maybe to go to the gym more as well, at some point.

You need to pose a challenge because nobody wants to date or be in a relationship with someone who is too compliant to everything, all the time. This is especially true in the case of men because they are "wired" to "fight" for their women—and sometimes, this might mean they are fighting their own instincts and habits.

Do not expect to *change* someone entirely, though. It's one thing to be a challenge intellectually or even physically. It's a completely different thing to want to change someone. It's unhealthy, it never works, and it always ends in pain on both ends.

## WHAT KIND OF CHALLENGE TO BE

OK, so we have established that you need to strike a balance between being a challenge and avoiding emasculating your date.

How do you do that?

Truth be told, it can be a little difficult to fine-tune yourself in this direction and that's mostly because everyone has their own point of balance when it comes to how they challenge others (in dating and otherwise).

A good example here is how different people manage their teams. You can always find people who manage their teams in an uplifting way, steering them in a direction of growth and self-confidence. And you will always find people who just boss people around and make them feel low.

Obviously, you want to be in the first category (always, not just when dating someone). Achieving that level of capability in managing your energies around the person you are dating takes time and practice, though. So you shouldn't put yourself down if you don't make it the first time around. Keep trying, we all have that indisputable point of balance within us, it just takes a little work finding it. Like riding a bike, though, once you have found it, you will always be able to rely on your instincts.

Going back to our discussion: what kind of challenge should you be?

Well, you should be the kind of challenge that stimulates a man, not emasculates him. That does not mean you should "play stupid" just to make sure your date isn't feeling "downgraded" when compared to you. That simply means you should pick your battles and know how to fight them.

You have to know how to use *challenge* to your benefit. As shown in the first section of this chapter, men enjoy a cerebral challenge during courtship, but it is also important to know that they enjoy being complimented on how many different areas they're knowledgeable in.

Obviously, you should only do this as you become closer (as it might come off as insincere if you do it at any other time). Oh, and by the way, if you don't find anything to genuinely compliment your date on, you should probably not be there as they are not a good match for you (and sooner or later, this will become an issue).

You should also fine-tune how you use your intelligence when you're around them. The so-called "battle of sexes" should be left at the door (preferably, at the door between the 20th and the 21st century, frankly).

This means you shouldn't use your intelligence combatively. Love is not a battlefield and your date is not a session of debate in school. You don't need to prove you're smarter than him; you just need to show him you're smart enough to pose some sort of cerebral challenge to him.

All humans are impressed by the effort it took to accomplish a goal. That's why we look up to athletes, for example. We know it takes a ton of hard work to become a professional athlete. Or a professional actor, painter, or a brilliant entrepreneur. We're not really impressed by anyone who got rich overnight by winning the lottery. We *are*, however, impressed by those who worked for their goal.

This stands just as true in dating too. How much a man values you is directly correlated to how much hard work they have put into actually winning you. If you're easy (and not just when it comes to sex, sorry), you'll only be perceived as a participation trophy. If you pose a challenge, you will be perceived as the gold medal.

Thus, the attitude you should assume is this: *if you can keep up with my life, then maybe you can be in it.* You should be a woman who's hard to get because you're on your own path and the pace is high. As such, men should see if they can fit in and match your velocity in your interests.

You, as a woman of high-value, have your own trajectory and your goals, and the men you date should show that they can thrive in what makes you unique. For instance, if you're in an indie music band, they should be able to show that, at a minimum, they can make it to your gigs as much as possible or find other ways to enhance your passion for your own trajectory. In any case, they should never try to pry you away from it just because you think they're cute.

The challenge your ideal man should meet is rising to the occasion of you and your life. Don't just *play* hard to get. **Be** hard to get because you're successful, because you believe in yourself and your path, because you will not settle for just anyone who comes along with a pair of pretty eyes, some nice pecs, and a couple of funny jokes. Those are all great, but if the person behind them is not ready to fully rise up to the challenge of you as a whole, they do not mean much.

## CONFIDENCE AND CHALLENGE

There's no challenge without confidence, and there's no true confidence without challenge. The two are interlinked and inseparable, especially for a Brilliant Vixen (but definitely not only for her, as it is applicable for every woman and man out there, both when it comes to dating and other areas of life).

Let us not digress though. Why is confidence such an integral part of being a challenge, and how do you use it to your advantage?

Confidence oozes through one's skin and makes the difference between a woman who's a challenge because she's absolutely amazing and the man wants to be with her and a woman who just "fakes" her image.

A woman shouldn't "play hard to get," instead they should "be hard to get." That's an important distinction that is often misunderstood, so ladies please take a minute to really internalize that. Time will always reveal the truth of all things so be genuinely hard to get and you'll never have to worry.

Let me go back to the sports example to showcase just how important confidence is. Several studies have shown that confidence plays a major role in how successful athletes are. In other words, "...athletes who possess a strong belief in their ability reported being able to peak under pressure and cope successfully with adverse situations during competition" (Hays et al., 2009).

It makes sense: when you are self-confident, your mindset is focused on succeeding and as such, your actions correlate with your thoughts. Competence breeds confidence, and confidence plays an essential role in gaining competence too. Just like confidence and challenge, competence and confidence are interlinked in an almost molecular way.

On the other hand, lack of confidence can also lead to tangible outcomes. "Confidence has been consistently associated with positive affect, whereas a lack of confidence has been associated with anxiety, depression, and dissatisfaction" (Hays et al., 2009).

It is important to note that your confidence should not be mirrored in an aggressive behavior. Being genuinely self-confident elicits respect in others (including the men you're dating). Being a show-off, on the other hand, will put off men (at the very least) or downright annoy them (which is also true for pretty much everyone else as well, not just the men you date).

So, how do you boost your self-confidence in a way that's healthy (and noticeably so)? Some tips to consider include the following:

- Take care of yourself. This includes your body and your mind. You don't have to fit into the sometimes ridiculous standards fashion imposes to look great and *feel* great in your own skin. What you do have to do, however, is work on it. Be physically active, eat food that makes you feel energized, and train your mind by reading, practicing mindfulness, and taking time off to relax. These are not things that will show an effect immediately, but week after week, month after month, you will feel like a whole new person. And it will be noticeable, especially by men who are worth your time.

- Change how you see yourself. We all have a mental image of how we look and how we are, but if our mental images and the language we use to describe ourselves are negative, that's exactly what we'll mirror on the outside. Work on changing the imagery and the language you mentally use to "see" yourself.

- Kill negative thoughts. Kill them soon and kill them ruthlessly. Whatever thought crosses your mind and puts you in the *"can't"* mentality is negative and it should be banished from your life.

- Be kind to others. Being kind and generous to others, helping those in need, and generally being good to people has positive effects not only on them, but on ourselves too. Of course, there's a limit and you should know where to draw the line in how good you are to those around you—but even little acts of generosity and kindness can actually boost your self-confidence, so try to include them in your life as much as possible.

- Learn and be prepared. Being a competent human being in any field does not just happen overnight. All those famous women shining their strength unto the world? They worked hard to get there. And no. it's never too late to start working hard on yourself. Start today and, one year from now, you'll be a thousand miles closer to your goal.

- Speak slowly. When you speak slowly and clearly but do not raise your voice too much, people lean in to listen. That boosts your self-confidence on multiple levels. For one, people are actually paying attention to you. Even more than that, you can take your time to choose just the right words and emanate a

sense of self-confidence in everything
you say.

- Set small goals. Yes, you should totally have bigger goals too. But smaller goals boost your self-confidence. Working out five days in a streak, learning how to make your own latte, submitting your work one day before the deadline—these are small, baby steps you can take to building yourself up.

- Change small habits. Do you wake up and jump to your coffee machine without even opening your eyes? Change that and insert a small habit before your morning coffee: a little bit of stretching or a positive affirmation or anything else small and positive. Of course, these are just examples. You can work into your life whatever other small habits you think are suitable for you.

- Smile. This is not about being the nice girl who always smiles. It's about setting yourself in a positive mindset. When you smile, your brain automatically sets itself up into "positive mode." Moreover, people smile back at you, which boosts your self-confidence from that point of view as well.

- Be grateful. Keeping a gratitude journal is a great way to banish negative thoughts away and build yourself on a positive mindset. Just write down whatever made you grateful every day or follow specific gratefulness journaling prompts, such as:

- Describing your favorite moment of the day
- Describing the wonderful people in your life
- Describing something uplifting that happened to you that day
- Describing a specific happy memory
- Describing what you love about your friends, family, etc.
- Take risks. No, this doesn't mean you should book the next bungee jumping session available. Instead, take smaller risks, such as getting on stage at a karaoke night. Build your way up to bigger risks, such as setting up a business or writing a book, or whatever other "crazy" goal you might have.
- Accept compliments. And do it gracefully. A simple "thank you, it means a lot" or "thank you, I worked hard for that" will do, you don't need to expand on how you think it would have looked better on someone else or on how someone else would have done it better.

All these things might not be directly related to dating or finding a point of balance between being a challenge and being *too much*. However, they will build on your personality and your strength. The right man will notice you are self-confident precisely because you have "exercised your confidence muscle" using small, yet meaningful practices such as those mentioned above.

## HOW TO BE MORE OF A CHALLENGE (THE RIGHT WAY)

Now that we have elaborated on why being a challenge is important and how it is connected to self-confidence, let's jump to specific examples. How can you be more of a challenge the right way?

### *Don't Become Too Invested, Too Soon*

People joke a lot about this, but being too invested very early in a relationship is the number one killer of challenge. And romance.

Yes, you might sense you want babies with a guy who meets all your standards (at least from afar). But letting him know that is a complete no-no, and you know it.

OK, that might have been an exaggerated example, but there are a lot of small things women do that show they're too invested, too soon. From letting them know you've scrolled down his Insta profile to the beginning of time to just talking too much about your family and even over-dressing for a date, there are a lot of "investment" cues men can actually pick up from you. Try to be conscious of them and avoid them, especially early in a relationship.

Men don't like these cues not because they're genetically programmed to be afraid of commitment, but because they eliminate the challenging side in winning your heart. If your heart and soul are already theirs, what do they have to work towards?

On top of all this over-investing in someone raises the level of scarcity you will feel, which puts tons of unnecessary pressure on this potential relationship.

### *Don't Over-Share*

It's not that you're not an interesting person or that your life is not absolutely fascinating. It's just that giving away too much about yourself can be:

- Tiresome, because there's a lot of information the person in front of you has to assimilate.
- A killer of romance and challenge. If you tell them everything, where's the playful discovery and where's the fun game for the man you're dating? Where's the hard work they're supposed to put into winning an amazing woman like you?

Give them nuggets of information that show that you are interesting and intelligent, but don't share the entire story of your life in two dates and ten random text messages. We will discuss more about mystery in Chapter 6, though.

### Don't Be Too Available

You don't always have to be available for dates when he wants it. This sends us right back to "becoming too invested, too soon" and it sends a very wrong message: you're there to do whatever this guy wants, whenever he wants it.

Play around, but do it in a fun and flirty way. Show them you have your own life, your own schedule, your own path and that you won't just toss everything out as soon as a cute guy comes along.

### Learn How to Verbally "Poke" Guys

This is also referred to as "sh*t-testing guys." Yes, the name leaves something to be desired, but it's basically about testing men to see if they're up to a light-hearted verbal challenge and if they have a metaphorical spine or not.

Keep in mind that there's a difference between cute "verbal pokes" and downright negging a guy. They like the first because it poses a challenge (and a fun one at that). They absolutely loathe the second because no man wants to get into a relationship where the woman is constantly annoying or degrading them.

"Negs" are naturally "designed" to undermine one's self-esteem, while intellectual challenges are just fun little games that make men's brains turn on and help you see how they reason.

### Examples of Being a Nice Challenge

Here are a couple of examples of how being a "nice challenge" can work, just to give you an idea of the kind of tone of voice and "games" you are looking for.

### Example 1:

Him: "I'd like to take you out for a drink."

Her: "Oh you would, wouldn't you? How do I know I'm going to have fun in this *get a drink situation?*"

### Example 2:

Him: "Your hair is beautiful; I've always loved brunettes."

Her: "So any brunette will do then?"

In both of these examples, the challenge is definitive: the guy has to be either charming and witty in how they answer her *or* they can choose to be uncomfortable, pouty, and angry. Either way, you win: you either get into a fun conversation that might turn into something deep and beautiful *or* you stop wasting your time on a guy who doesn't deserve your time and your worth.

*Do* keep in mind that when you're "verbally poking" someone, you have to pay attention to non-verbal cues as well. If these are in-person conversations, remember to give the guy a coy smile when you deliver the "test." If this is texting, use a "thinking" or a "wink" emoji to show you're just being playful and flirty.

Being a challenge might not always come natural, but it should in no way be a challenge to *you*. As I mentioned earlier in this chapter, we all have it in us. All it takes is a little practice to bring out the best in you that shows men you're the *great* kind of challenge.

The kind that helps *them* grow and makes them happy every day of their lives.

The kind that brings joy and wit into a relationship.

The kind that makes things better than "nice," more like incredibly giddy-level excitedly amazing, every step of the way!

*Chapter Six*

# MYSTERY

"You know what's the sexiest thing of all? A little mystery."

— RAQUEL WELCH (WELCH, N.D.)

S how me someone who doesn't enjoy mystery and I'll prove to you that they're either lying or completely narrowing down the meaning of "mystery" altogether.

We are inherently attracted to mystery, just like bees are attracted to pollen and children to everything that shines bright. We're built to seek mystery and feed on it every day of our lives.

Some do it by committing to spiritual journeys that quench their thirst for mystery.

Others do it by adventuring around the world every opportunity they get.

Others experience mystery by constantly seeking themselves.

Most of us get little doses of mystery from the everyday things, like movies and books (because, yes, even when they're not labeled "mystery" or "thriller," they are still tapping into our need to be close to mystery). You want to let the mystery that is your life unfold organically in a natural rhythm, instead of blurting it out all at once which is like reading an article full of spoilers before you watch the movie.

People who say they like everything to be crystal clear and that they don't enjoy mystery at all are only looking at the *facade* of what mystery involves. Under the influence of a Hollywood action movie-based civilization, it seems that all we can automatically associate with mystery are ghosts, secret fantasy relics, and murder thrillers.

Sure, those can very well qualify as mysteries too. But so is Yoga or Tai-Chi, or meditation. So is opening a book and not knowing exactly what to expect to find between the pages. So is jumping into a new career opportunity or taking on a daring project unlike anything you've managed before.

Mystery runs through our veins and we'll always seek it. I'll bet you that four centuries from now, when we travel between planets and galaxies, people will still be seeking mystery. Because why else would they even adventure out there, then?

Science, literature, poetry, arts, music, philosophy— literally every field we've ever "invented" tries to get a slice of the whole pie called "mystery."

Some try to solve the mystery (like, for example, how physicians these days are trying to reconcile traditional physics and quantum mechanics).

Others, on the other hand, bask in the glory and beauty of mystery. Philosopher Kierkegaard is famous for having said that "Life is not a problem to be solved, but a mystery to be experienced" (Kierkegaard, n.d.). And pretty much every writer, poet, artist, or musician in history has somehow tried to explain mysteries without crushing them with finite answers.

The point is that we love mystery because it goes straight to who we are, as living beings inhabiting the planet called Earth.

'A sense of mystery is intrinsic to the human mind,' says Les Lancaster, professor of transpersonal psychology at Liverpool John Moores University. 'It's intrinsic for us to seek answers. It's our evolutionary heritage, moving us forward by motivating us to find out more and use our imagination.' Mystery is the ultimate trail of breadcrumbs. It piques our interest, invites us to solve or make sense of something and use our imagination to fill in the gaps. (Taylor, 2010)

## WHY IS MYSTERY IMPORTANT IN DATING?

Imagine the ultimate femme fatale, the James Bond pair, the walking embodiment of mystique in six-inch stilettos. The woman who confidently walks into a bar in a film noir, orders a dry scotch, and enjoys it at the bar, alone, while every man in the room wants to approach her.

You might think femme fatales only belong in movies, and even more so, that they're a bygone species of an even more bygone era.

Nothing could be more inaccurate, though. The femme fatale archetype is still very much among us, in movies and books, in art, and in how musicians pose in front of the world. Just look at lethal super-hero Zoe Saldana from Guardians of The Galaxy, supermodel turned action superstar Milla Jovovich's entire career, DC comic books' number one villain Harley Quinn, or Helen Mirren in "Red" taking out bad guys with the utmost poise and charm. Femme fatals come in all shapes, sizes, backgrounds, and age ranges so there's an icon for everyone.

Even more than that, men are just as fascinated with this archetype as they have ever been. The reason is simple: all human beings love mystery, but there's nothing more enticing for a man than a woman who hides little, beautiful secrets and does not uncover her entire self from the first date.

Mystery is a very potent attractor. A mysterious woman is an instant cut above any other woman around her because in a man's eyes, she is hard to pigeonhole. Women who don't fit neatly in a box are those that are most attractive in men's eyes, precisely because they capture their imagination.

There's a lot more innate logic to this type of behavior than most people give it credit for. We, humans, are a very curious species. Our curiosity is one of the qualities that helped us rise to the top of the food chain, even though we did not possess the fastest legs, the fiercest fangs, or the most imposing stature.

The fact that we've always been curious and resilient helped us find solutions—and this is particularly true in the case of men, who, by a still unknown set of circumstances and in most societies, were the ones forced to find the most cutting-edge solutions to provide for their communities and families.

As such, humans (and particularly men) are more inclined to pursue mystery until they find a satisfactory answer. If you are a mystery to the man you're dating and he can't put you in a box, he will be a lot more interested in wanting to see more of you.

Going back to our James Bond example, do you know why the idea of a secret agent is so intriguing for everyone? We're most definitely not attracted to the fact that they lie and steal to get what they want. We are, however, attracted to a fantastical life we can't put our finger on, but know it's not boring.

Boredom is the death of curiosity, and that is exactly why men will obsess about finding someone who is interesting and coyly elusive. Which is precisely the type of "mystery" you should be for them.

Walk a mile in a guy's shoes to understand why they are so eager to find women who stir their curiosity.

Most men have had similar experiences on dates, and most likely on more than one occasion. The woman does "x" for a living, has a "y" for a pet, and had a hard week at work getting stuck in traffic.

Sure, ladies who share this kind of stuff on dates are probably just nervous or venting and they forget they should be leading with their best foot forward. However, by doing all this and not taking control over their "mystery," they are making a grave error, because this kind of banter is a real attraction killer. Don't get lost in a sea of forgettable women, avoid complaining about the mundane, and avoid fitting into any kind of box, especially when you're on your first dates with someone.

The reason "Bond Girls" are so intriguing to men is because they are very hard to figure out. They live the kind of lives they couldn't tell you about in one sitting, even if they chose too. They strike the perfect balance between being flirtatious and emotionally reserved, slightly playful, but never to be taken lightly. They only allow the best of the best to even bother attempting to gain their company.

Obviously, I'm not suggesting you should join the CIA or strike up an association with a colorful super-villain to become intriguing in men's eyes. That's *a little* bit too much just for the attention of men.

What I *am* suggesting, though, is the best life advice you'll ever receive: have a rich life full of interests that you pursue. Design a life you find enriching and rewarding regardless of whether or not you're dating someone.

Explore new hobbies that kick you out of the house and make you feel excited and alive. Do things *for you*, not because they're interesting in the eyes of society (or, Heavens forbid, because they might seem interesting for men).

Improve the quality of your life first. Boost your level of happiness and allow your vibration to grow with you. Little by little, new, amazing people will walk into your life, attracted like magnets to your mystery.

Learn how to stay in the moment, as opposed to talking about negative past experiences. If you're hung up on your past and keep talking about it, you're killing the mystery—and together with it, your personal appeal as well.

Think of how you react around guys who possess no mystery at all. Your average "nice guy" will give you everything about him after the first date. Spending just a couple of hours with this guy will make you feel like you know *everything* about him. Hell, you can even anticipate what they're going to say next, and that's exactly when you realize all the mystery is officially gone.

The butterflies are dead, the attraction you have towards this person who has revealed everything about them is running on low-battery mode, and frankly, there's not much they could do at this point to recharge the attraction-o-meter in your eyes.

It's gone.

And that's exactly the kind of person you **don't** want to be when you date someone. You want to give them little nuggets about who you are and what you do, you want to entice them and engage in interesting conversations, you want to create an aura of mystique around you.

No, you don't need to have a female supervillain's past to do that. You can just work on building up skills and knowledge in topics that enhance who you **truly** are on a day to day basis. It could be martial arts, comic book knowledge, reading books, skydiving, singing—anything you genuinely enjoy doing.

The whole point in building *yourself* up is that the things you're doing to grow are not easily observable (unless you bring papyrus scrolls to your dates, listing every little thing you've ever done and tried, which you probably don't do). As such, these little things become the brick and mortar of your personal sense of mystery.

For example, if you like the outdoors and your car is covered in hiking stickers, you've killed the mystery about that. But if you have also been learning how to play the violin and you have your first gig coming up soon, that's something unexpected and not easily observable. Therefore, it makes you mysterious in your unique way.

You should never copy anyone else's mystery. You don't have to walk on six-inch stiletto heels or wear tight red dresses all the time. You don't have to like scotch, or even sport lush blond curls.

You have to be yourself, but a version of yourself that doesn't show everything and yet *works* on everything in the background. Although not obvious to the eye, these things can be sensed, and they are a key ingredient in making yourself irresistible for men.

## HOW TO HAVE MORE MYSTERY

Evidently, you can't order more mystery online, nor can you find it on discount at the mall.

Having more mystery is all about the work you put into yourself to make yourself happy. It sounds a little counterintuitive, because most people associate mystery with thrillers (as we have already discussed in the introduction to this chapter).

However, it is exactly what you need. You build mystery around yourself when you do things that enhance who you are, be it an artistic side of you that you may not have shown to everyone or a very pragmatic one, like how you are secretly working on starting your own business.

Of course, sooner or later, the man you're dating will find out about these little (or not so little) things that define the "you" in the "background." But before you get there, you should learn how to allude to your mystery and create an aura of uniqueness around you.

Here are some ways to do this:

- Be curious. The more curious you are, the more unique your interests will be. Most men don't expect someone who doesn't work in science to be interested in, for example, quantum physics. But if you are and you leave him with just a very interesting nugget of information based on your latest quantum physics read, you will baffle him just enough to make him want to ask for more.
- Pursue your interests out of the house too. Reading and obscure movies are perfectly

fine, but having a couple of talents that "happen" outside of the house can make a real difference.

- Build unique skills. It doesn't have to be something useful per se, but make sure it's something you genuinely enjoy doing and which you can get fairly good at.

- Avoid talking about all your interests or skills, and when you do it, be a little playful and coy about it. Most definitely **do not** share everything about you at once, even if you share a little piece of one of your interests.

- Reveal skills on fun dates without warning him about what you can do. If he is a little shocked at your hidden talents, you've done a great job because it will leave him wondering what other hidden skills or talents you have that you haven't told him about. As such, he will be blindsided by talent, and you will force his brain into "curiosity mode" (where he genuinely wants to find out more about you).

- When you show your talents and skills, always make sure you're not doing it in a patronizing or overly confident way. Remember, you want to be the good kind of challenge, not the kind of challenge that makes guys feel low (refer back to Chapter 5 for more information on this).

What are some interesting hobbies or skills you could pursue, for example? Frankly, it can be anything as long as it's not the kind of interest every other woman and their grandma have. Some examples of great hobbies you can try to include:

- Archery (I bet he won't suspect this one)
- Reading poetry at an open mic night (which shows your courage to be emotionally vulnerable in front of an audience and still be incredibly strong and in control while doing it)
- Singing or playing an instrument (just imagine his face when, at karaoke, you actually own the stage and the audience!)
- Rock climbing (because what can ever be more attractive than a woman who can literally conquer mountains?)
- Painting at an art and wine night or even working on making your artistic work public in a gallery (there will always be a special mystique surrounding artists, right?)
- Making pottery (we all know the movie scenes, and we know that's exactly what he'll imagine too)

- Winning trivia games at bars (keep it playful, though, this should not make your date feel bad about their own knowledge or lack of competitive spirit)
- Playing board games or video games and being absolutely amazing at it (because, let's face it, most men don't expect a lady to expertly maneuver the mouse and the keyboard in Counter Strike, for example).

Whatever you choose, make sure there's an element of surprise to it. Even more, make sure you don't reveal it all at once. So if you show him you're talented at singing when you attend a karaoke party together, don't mention the fact that you've been taking singing lessons for years now, nor do you mention the fact that you used to be in a girl band in high school). Keep in mind this should not be about keeping secrets, it's more about saving surprises. When I explained the difference to my daughter I told her "Secrets are things which will upset the person when they find out. Surprises will make them smile when you share them."

The more breadcrumbs you can get out of your hobby or skill, the more it will help you become more mysterious in your date's eyes. And that is exactly what you want.

## WHAT KILLS MYSTERY AND HOW TO AVOID IT

No matter how much mystery you build around yourself, keep in mind that you can always kill it with small, apparently insignificant mistakes. A lot of women fall into this trap: they are absolutely amazing in a million and one ways, but they make a wrong move and end up killing their own auras of mystique.

There are many such blunders you can inadvertently step into (so many it would probably take an entirely different book to talk about all of them). However, if we have to narrow them down to the absolute basics, here are the four things you should always avoid doing:

- Complaining. This is the absolute King and Queen of all mystery killers. The Jason Voorhees meets Freddy Kruger of everything that could ever absolutely murder your aura of mystique. Most women don't think complaining is that bad, but the absolute truth is this: it is. Complaining is mundane and boring, and it puts you in a little box in a man's eyes (the box that says "Boring, nagging, snooze-fest of a life").

Don't complain. There's nothing interesting about it, and you're not bringing out any kind of savior in the man you're complaining to (mostly because there's nothing he can do about bad jobs, bad meals, and bad traffic).

There are literally a billion things you could talk about. Take each of them one by one and leave complaining for number 1,000,000,0001.

- Over-sharing. This one's pretty obvious: when you start sharing too many details about yourself, you risk sharing everything. And the next thing that happens is him getting bored of you because you have killed all the mystique.

Keep in mind: not being over-sharing does not mean you shouldn't answer his questions when he's genuinely interested. It just means you should know how to calibrate how much of the "BIG" answer you give him.

Conversation should be a game of ping-pong, not Hamlet's monologue (which is amazing and we all love it, but it has no room in dating, same as any other type of monologue). If you monopolize the conversation, he'll literally think you're not interested in him and as such, his interest in you will drop significantly too (remember what we talked about in Chapter 2?).

- Wearing your heart on your sleeve. Showing someone you like them too much is dangerous because it will kill the mystery (not to mention that it opens the doors to them taking advantage of your open-heartedness, in the worst case scenarios).

Nobody says you should be a constant riddle and that you should always hide your emotions at any cost. Again, this is a matter of calibration and how much of yourself you choose to share (verbally or not).

For example, if you want to let a guy know you like him, flirting is a much better alternative than straight-up staring at him with stars in your eyes and growing hope in your look (an obvious exaggeration, but you get the point here).

- Not having any other facets aside from what you do for a living. If all you are is work, work, work, all you do is probably bore him (even if he works in the same field as you do). Once the office door closes behind them, most people want to escape the very topic of work, so try not to talk about it the entire evening.

Yes, you can definitely tell him what you do for a living. And yes, you can even show you're passionate about what you do. But if you don't have any significant interests outside of work, he will not perceive you as interesting—and soon enough, all the curiosities he has about you will die a sudden death.

I know all this sounds a bit harsh. It is nothing but the truth, though. Creating mystery is a matter of self-control and knowing how to tell your story to men with little bits and pieces of the best of you. Like it or not, it's part of the game, just like dice are part of Monopoly and guns are part of Counter Strike.

Play this move correctly and you've won his long-term interest.

**In the pursuit of mystery, we cultivate our best selves.**

Which brings us to the seventh element of our Brilliant Vixen iceberg...

*Chapter Seven*

# CONSTANTLY EVOLVING

"Look around you. Everything changes. Everything on this earth is in a continuous state of evolving, refining, improving, adapting, enhancing, and changing. You were not put on this earth to remain stagnant."

— DR. STEVE MARABOLI
(MARABOLI, 2009)

I t is safe to assume that all (or most) of the elements we have discussed in the book so far are more or less familiar to you:

- You always knew guys like fun girls

- You probably noticed that flirty women are more attractive
- You also most likely knew being genuine is really important for attraction
- You sensed that being high-value is crucial
- You have been told that you should challenge the men you're dating
- You have always known there's a fascination for mysterious women

All these are things women either know intuitively or have been encouraged by other women to practice. Most women do not know exactly how to pull them off, but hopefully, the book at hand has helped you gain a better understanding of why exactly all these elements are important and how to let them shine so you attract **the right kind of man for you**.

However, what we're about to discuss in this chapter is not as intuitive. Of course, I am certain many of you will know the importance of doing it, but not necessarily how it connects to dating (and even more so, dating men actually worth your time).

As the title of this chapter suggests it, the last element in our Brilliant Vixen iceberg is making sure you are constantly evolving. Obviously, this brings benefits outside of the dating "field" as well. It changes how you see life, how you see yourself, how you relate to the less pleasant events you stumble upon, how you work to achieve your goals, and even how you move and how you eat. It goes down into your cellular levels and changes you in the best way there is.

I cannot emphasize enough just how important it is for you to strive for constant evolution, and I'm not even doing it because I think it's important when it comes to attracting good men. With or without a man in your life, aiming to constantly "upgrade" yourself will give your life meaning and substance—and isn't that just what life is all about, in the end?

We're not here to discuss the meaning of life, though, and I know that. We're here to discuss how you can become an absolutely irresistible woman and how the "constant evolution" part is the last piece of the puzzle you're starting to build right now, reading this book.

So, what is this whole constant evolution thing all about?

## WHY CONSTANT EVOLUTION MATTERS IN DATING

You wouldn't be automatically inclined to believe something like personal growth directly affects your dating life. But it does, and greatly so.

Your fun side attracts men, your flirty side lets them know you like them, being genuine shows them you are a real person who is confident in herself, being high-value shows them you're not here to waste your time or theirs, and being mysterious makes them curious to see more of you.

Constant evolution is the missing ingredient, the one that makes a great man want to *stay* with you for a long period of time precisely because you are constantly reinventing yourself.

In other words, constant evolution is a state of perpetual "mystery." If being a little mysterious is enough to stir a man up and make them find you truly interesting, being focused on constant evolution maintains that state past the first dates. There's just no other better way to do it: if you want to maintain that state of "mystery" you're creating when you first start dating a guy, you have to be in constant evolution. That way you're continually adding new chapters to the book of you for him to discover.

Note I am using the word "evolution" and not "change," and there's an important semantic idea to keep in mind here. Change is not always for the better, and it also involves you becoming someone else at least in certain respects. Evolution, on the other change, means you are consistently upgrading yourself.

So why is all this important?

Because it deepens a man's fascination with you. When you constantly work on yourself to be better, you show men you're strong, confident, and smart in the best way there is. You're not diminishing his skills, qualities, or personality. You shine on your own and you do not need to put someone else down to do so. You become an eternally fascinating person he always comes back to mentally.

You see, being an incredibly irresistible woman has little to do with size, looks, or the type of clothes you want to wear. Sure, a well-groomed appearance shows you care and it shows you're confident. But beyond all that, it is your *mind* he wants most. If the man you're seeing is worth your time, he will fall in love with the *you* that goes on beyond the physical body.

Again—and I really want to emphasize this because a lot of people get this in a distorted way—you should always aim to make a man fall in love with your brain, rather than your body. But that does not necessarily mean you can let yourself go, simply because it's not the smart, nor the healthy way to deal with yourself (not at a mental level, and not at a physical level either).

Constant evolution helps you make sure your interesting side does not necessarily have a finite part to it. When you work on yourself all the time and better yourself, you will never stagnate, and as such, there will always be interesting things about you.

When you continue to grow and evolve as a person, you'll be the opposite of the cliché popular girl who peaked in high school. This keeps the spark in your life and relationships and helps you avoid the common scenario where one of the partners in a couple "outgrows" the other.

Even more, when you work on yourself, you will naturally motivate a man to do the same as well, because he'll want to keep up with you without you forcing it into him. He'll want to be better and better, and together, you will become an unbeatable force of nature.

It sounds a little fantastical and movie-like, but that is exactly how successful long-term couples do it. I cannot guarantee "forever," and nobody in the whole wide world can do that. What I can guarantee is that when you get on top of the Brilliant Vixen iceberg, your relationships will be mind-blowingly amazing.

And you know why that is?

Because *you*, as an individual, will be absolutely awe-inspiring from every single point of view.

## EVERYTHING YOU EVER WANTED TO KNOW ABOUT SAPIOSEXUALITY

Being attracted to someone's mind and intellect has a name: sapiosexuality. According to the Macmillan Dictionary, a sapiosexual is "someone who is attracted by another person's intellect." It sounds very simple in essence, but the meaning behind the word is a little more complex when you get close to it.

You might have heard this word before, but the very harsh truth about it is that people have started tossing it around like it's nothing. Every other girl labels herself as sapiosexual like it's a hair-color, but the vast majority of people are nothing but the surface of sapiosexuality.

What these people are doing well, however, is intuitively knowing that someone who's a sapiosexual has great value to them, and this is particularly true in the case of men, who are stereotypically "planted" in boxes that say "he is only attracted to good looks."

A man who doesn't care that much about how long your legs are, what size your bra is, or how well-rounded your behind is, is a quality man. Sure, quality men *are* attracted to women who look good. But the "good looks" of these women go beyond ridiculous body and beauty standards.

Quality men know that kind of beauty is fading, but that the elegance of an intelligent woman who carries herself well is never-ending. Quality men will absolutely seek smart women who keep the flame alive not only through glossy magazine tricks for the bedroom, but through intelligent conversation and a genuine inclination towards bettering themselves.

You may or may not be a sapiosexual. I am not here to discuss taste. What I am here to say is that you should aim for the sapiosexual man. Don't be the object of any guy's passing physical desire, be the one who stirs up his mind and makes him want you for the amazing human being you are on every level.

How do you know when someone is a sapiosexual, for example? While most men don't just run around with "sapiosexual" tattooed on their biceps, there are some signs that someone falls in this category of attraction:

- They don't jump into a relationship without wanting to discover more about the *person* in front of them.
- They avoid and even explicitly say they hate

small talk. They would be much, much happier with an interesting conversation, so they might even challenge you to think of things you don't normally think about.

- They are not attracted to arrogant twits, but people who show signs of compassion, empathy, and a deep understanding of other people (all of which are signs of intelligence, by the way).

- They are excellent communicators. They will take their time texting you and you will smile at just how well-articulated their messages are, and just how much they tap into your desire to be with someone who is truly high-value (just like you are).

- They will straight up compliment your brain. While they definitely know how to compliment a dress that looks good on you, sapiosexuals will also know how to compliment how your thought process "functions."

- They will motivate you to grow. They will not do this in a way that feels invasive and abusive, but in a way that genuinely boosts your appetite for more knowledge, more skill, more intelligence, and more beauty (in an artistic sense). A sapiosexual will be so amazing to be around that you will naturally want to grow alongside them; and you, as a person who is constantly evolving, will be the object of their motivation to grow as well.

Of course, people are complex beings and you can't fit them all in little boxes that label them one way or another. Sapiosexuality is, however, the one spice that makes relationships the kind that makes for great stories.

## SIGNS YOU ARE EVOLVING AS A PERSON

"Evolved people change the world. They live happier, simpler, and more productive lives. The best part is, as you grow in consciousness, you can see these evidences in your life—confirming you are becoming the person you were meant to be."
Benjamin Hardy (Hardy, 2015)

Many people believe constant evolution feels more like a chore or a struggle, rather than something that gives them satisfaction. But that's not how it needs to be. Evolving as a person can give you satisfaction, and it's the kind of pleasure that cannot be compared to anything else.

Some signs that you're growing as a person include:

- You know who you are. Many people take "knowing themselves" quite lightly, but the absolute truth is that it takes hard work to know yourself in the real sense of the word. When you are evolving, you start getting a good sense of who you are, where you come from, and where you are going.

- You know what you want. People who work on themselves are less likely to get "lost" in a myriad of options. They know what they want and maybe even more importantly, they know how to go after it.

- You feel you're in the right place in life. You don't fight your "destiny" anymore. Regardless of what job you might have, where you might live, or whether or not you're seeing someone, you know you're in the perfect place and that things will only get better from now on.

- You feel like you can control your life. When you're constantly evolving, your life stops being a mystery driven by chaos, chance, and other people. You feel like you can truly control where you are going (and this stems from the fact that you know very well where you are) and adapt to changing circumstances while still staying on track.

- You set your own terms. You don't blindly

follow rules just because someone else put them there. You set your own book of terms and you follow it. Even more, you find within you the power to set the boundaries that others respect.

- You feel you have significantly simplified your life. Every day becomes cleaner and clearer. Yes, you work hard, and yes, you always strive for more. But deep down, there's a clarity to what you're doing, and you love it.

- You start manifesting goals more quickly. When you constantly evolve, you start manifesting goals more quickly. "I will someday write a book" becomes "I will write a book by the end of the year," and you start actually working towards making your goals come true.

- The right people just start coming into your life. You stop searching for the right people. Because you're in the right places and because mentally you're very well-balanced and strong in your position, the right people simply start appearing in your life.

- You feel that good luck and miracles actually do happen often. And that is mostly because you stop believing they're just happenstances, but the norm—and that you control them one way or another through action, goal-seeking, and a positive mentality.

- You take time to meditate every day. This doesn't mean you have to actually practice meditation. It just means that, at the end of each day, you take some time to think about the things that happened. You learn your lessons, internalize them, and take them with you to a whole new day.

- You don't waste your time. When you work on yourself, your time becomes precious. You know your priorities and you know how to use your 24 hours to your best advantage. Suddenly, negative people, time-wasters, and social media just don't mean as much to you, and you start to withdraw yourself from these sources of wasted time.

- Every day brings you closer to the future you really want. More importantly, you genuinely feel it. You can reach out and almost touch your path to success because you see it before you very clearly.

- You feel a gap growing between you and your old social groups. It's not that you're mean or that you think you're better than them. It's just that these people and social groups are not compatible with who you are anymore.

And you naturally fall apart from them, for your own good.

- You actively and intuitively seek change. You don't seek change just for the sake of it, nor does it feel like a forced process. You seek change the same way you drink water when you're thirsty: it becomes your nature.

- Taking risks doesn't scare you. In fact, it brings you joy. You know a good challenge when you see it and you are happy to jump into it knowing that at the very best, it will get you what you want and at the very least, it will teach you an important lesson.

- You start seeing the truth, even through the clouds. You stop falling for lies and make-believe because you now possess the clarity of someone who knows how multi-faceted things are and who has a deep understanding of herself and others as well.

- You become more conscious of what you eat. And you don't do it because some health guru on Instagram dictates it. You do it because it's exactly what your body is craving, knowing it needs to support you in a healthy, sustainable way.

- You start caring about people more, but you care less and less about what they think of you. You want to help people and you are very action-focused when it comes to this. At the same time, people's labels of you stop having any kind of meaning, precisely because you know who you are, where you are, and where you're going.

- You stop comparing yourself to others and start comparing your perpetually "new self" to your "old self." Nothing good ever came out of comparing oneself with others. Everything great that's ever happened in the history of mankind was the result of a constant "fight" against one's own limitations. As someone who is constantly evolving, you know this very, very well.

- You sincerely want others to succeed as well. Because you stop comparing yourself to others, you also stop holding grudges or being envious of them. You want everyone to succeed because, as we have already mentioned it earlier in the book, you genuinely believe there's an infinite amount of success to go around, and everyone can get a slice of it.

As you can see, constant evolution is not about others or the men that walk into your life. It is not about knowing how to "play" men better. It's all about working on yourself, being happy with yourself, and allowing the nature of things to work for you by rewarding you with good people in your life.

Birds of a feather *do* flock together, and they do so in the most natural and beautiful way there is.

## HOW TO EVOLVE AS A PERSON

There are a thousand and one ways to evolve as a person and frankly, nobody can give you a recipe on how you can do it. Neither can I, no matter how much I'd like to.

Evolving as a person is a personal experience. It is a path you find on your own (and a path you mostly follow on your own as well). It is hard work you do with yourself, more than anyone else in the world.

Indeed, I cannot give you a clear recipe and I most definitely cannot draw *your* path to personal growth. What I can do, however, is give you some examples of things you can do to facilitate growing in a healthy way.

### *Take a Class*

It doesn't even matter that much what kind of class you take. It can be something like crochet techniques on Skillshare or a course on digital marketing on Udemy. It can also be buying a subscription for

MasterClass, for example (which, by the way, is a great investment from my point of view).

You might not become a master in the given topic of your class, but it will surely give you a lot of new, interesting topics for conversation. Good classes will teach you something new and they will enable you to have conversations on fascinating topics (and talk about them with experience).

### Read More Books

Reading is one of the healthiest things you can do for yourself. Not only will fiction reading immerse you in amazing new worlds and broaden your emotional horizons, but reading any kind of book will stimulate your brain activity, help you be more empathetic, pay better attention, and generally be a better person. This is valid for both fiction and non-fiction reading.

### Trying Yoga

Yoga is a great exercise for the body and for the mind. You don't have to twist yourself in the oddest poses to reap all the benefits this ancient practice has to offer. You just have to pick your class, attend it with regularity, and aim to be better and better every day. It will train your body, improve your posture, help you stretch out better, and it will train your mind to stay motivated and focused too. What more could you want?

### Start Meditating

Just like Yoga, meditation is an ancient Oriental practice. And just like Yoga, meditation relies on training the brain to stay focused. Yes, most types of meditation do not include physical exercise, but even so, meditation is a practice based on constant evolution in its purest form. This is precisely why it's a great endeavor to add to your list of personal growth.

### Learning a Foreign Language

It doesn't matter if it's Russian, French, Mandarin Chinese, or Arabic.

Every new language opens your mind and your heart to a new culture, to a new way of thinking. Learning new languages trains your mind, your memory, your focus, your motivation, and your empathy "muscle."

Even more than that, knowing a different language makes you interesting in the eyes of others. It gives you great topics of conversation. And ultimately, it is the kind of thing you can do for yourself to make yourself feel better and better.

### Learn Martial Arts

Not only are martial arts great for self-defense, but they are also a great exercise for the mind. Because they rely so much on self-control (both at a physical and at a mental level), martial arts are a perfect exercise for those looking to better themselves.

Plus, practicing martial arts can also open you up to a new culture and allow you to gain a deeper understanding of how they think.

### Go Skydiving

OK, this might be for the brave ones, but skydiving is the kind of thing that the kind of thing that can get your adrenaline going and feel more alive than ever. Doing something like this shows you're bold and courageous—and it definitely makes for very interesting conversations.

### Try an Art Party

Art parties involve painting with friends and drinking wine (or anything else you like, really). You don't even have to be extremely skilled at it, you just have to do it. These kinds of things broaden your horizons, help you cope with your emotions, and frankly, have fun in a smart and beautiful way.

### Take up Belly Dancing

There's something irresistible about a woman who can dance, and even more so a woman who practices belly dancing, a type of dance that's charged with eroticism, beauty, and grace.

Like any other exercise, belly dancing will not only help you become more in touch with your body, but also learn something new about the world and about yourself. It's the perfect material for personal growth, really!

### *Go Hiking*

Most men don't associate women with hiking, so this will be a nice surprise for most of the guys you'll date.

More importantly than that, hiking is the kind of activity that allows you to test and exceed your limits. Hiking also fosters personal growth through connecting to nature, which results in feeling more grounded at a psychological and physical level as well.

### *Pick a Random Experience on Groupon*

Immersing yourself in a random enjoyable experience makes you fun, interesting, mysterious, and it shows you're always open to grow and try new things. And when it comes to this last part, you can rest assured that you'll always find new, exciting, and fun things to do with your time, especially on platforms like Groupon for example.

I mean, you can literally get chased by zombies in a Groupon experience, so don't tell me there's nothing new for you there!

### Travel More

Frankly, the most consistent game-changer in my personal evolution has always been international travel. Seeing a completely new part of the world changes the way you think (and in very positive ways). It's a complete shift in perspective and gets you to question why you do things the way you do at home. There's literally no downside to traveling. In the worst case scenario, you'll gain some great new stories and a new appreciation for things you might take for granted at home.

If international travel isn't in your budget, keep in mind that even a road trip in your own home country can yield some pretty amazing results. In the end, the open road is always full of stories waiting to be told!

What do all these activities have in common?

They all get you out of your comfort zone, which is where major growth will happen. Just like everything else, constantly evolving is a **choice** you make, and you should always ask yourself if what you're about to do is in alignment with your life goals.

On average, our bodies completely renew themselves at a cellular level every 10 years. Some changes happen from one second to the other, while other changes take several years.

The deep YOU should be in tune with your body too. Seek to constantly change and evolve, to be better, to gain new experiences, and live life to the fullest in the most beautiful sense of the word.

---

**"The privilege of a lifetime is to become who you truly are." - Carl Jung** ("A Quote by C. G. Jung, n.d.-b)

---

# Chapter Eight

# THE CRYSTAL BALL: THE FUTURE OF MISSING ELEMENTS

*"Inaction breeds doubt and fear. Action breeds confidence and courage. If you want to conquer fear, do not sit at home and think about it. Go out and get busy"*

— DALE CARNEGIE ("A QUOTE BY DALE CARNEGIE," N.D.)

Here we are, at the end of our journey in this book. As we moved from the tip of the Brilliant Vixen iceberg to its foundation, I hope my words have helped you discover the right path for you to take from here on.

I chose to add one last chapter to this book to emphasize just how important each and every element described here is for your success. Yes, some elements might lie at the tip of the iceberg and some may go deeper, but they are all equally essential to making you an irresistible woman—and even more than that, a woman who attracts excellent men.

To help you visualize the importance of each of the individual elements described in this book, let's play a little game and imagine scenarios where the woman is missing out on *one* of them at a time.

Step into my fortune-teller booth and I'll show you how life would look like if you nailed everything perfectly, except for just one of the individual pieces!

## NOT BEING FUN

This is a woman who is high-quality from every point of view, but she tends to be a little bit on the boring side (OK, a lot). She will max out as a dependable wife who's left waiting at home and for whom a fun new lady that comes along poses a real threat.

## NOT BEING FLIRTY

This could be a person who is super-successful, an over-achiever by definition. A woman like this who is not flirty will tend to be annoyed with men because they'd much rather date her personal assistant than her.

This is a great woman by all means, but there's little chance of romance for a man to get swept up in. Most likely, she will end up being friend-zoned.

## NOT BEING GENUINE

We've all met this type at least once in our life. This is the woman who, at some level, either pretends to be something she thinks a guy would like or thinks she can trick a guy into falling in love with her. The reason she does this is actually painfully simple: she doesn't think she's good enough.

Her self-esteem is pretty low and it shows as a façade. It's hard to actually get to know this woman at all in a real sense—so why would anyone truly fall in love with her when they don't even know her (the real her)?

The extreme version of this type thinks her love interest is her opponent. As such, she feels she needs to defeat her partner in order for him to love her. This girl will say things like "He thinks he's slick, but girl, I've got more game than Milton-Bradley" (and yes, sadly, this is a real-life conversation with a girl who was pretty, fit, but lacked self-esteem. She also lacked the ability to not get played by bad-boys).

At best, this woman is trying to be something she's not. At worst, she's a serial manipulator who should be very, very afraid of karma.

Sadly, a lot of times, this woman ends up in scenarios where her boyfriend/partner slept with her best friend.

## NOT BEING HIGH-VALUE

This woman is always feeling "used" by men. She's a mistress, not a one-and-only. Her curse is watching her ex-boyfriends marry the next woman they date after her. She's not giving men any reason to treat her well, so she'll end up consistently attracting men who will not. I'm not particularly fond of these words, but women in this category are very easily categorized as "booty calls" or "side chicks."

## NOT BEING A CHALLENGE

This girl will drop *everything* the second a guy is remotely interested in her. She will cancel your girls' night out indefinitely, she will stop going to Yoga unless it's during a time he's busy, and she'll even wait for a guy to finish *his* guys' night out to have a "date."

This woman can also come off as clingy. She'll bring a guy lunch at work after they've been dating for a week and she's tremendously eager to introduce him to her parents. Because of behaviors like this, he's not going to commit to her because it feels like a trap for his future joy.

If it weren't for her clinginess, this woman would have easily been seen as a "booty call" or "side chick" too. Most guys feel that she's too needy to be kept around for very long in any capacity. If she is kept around, it's only as a placeholder to be used as needed, for the time being.

When this woman dates someone long-term, she usually ends up wondering why she wasted so much time when the relationship turns out to be a dead end.

## NOT HAVING MYSTERY

This is the girl who spills her guts out on a first date and tells men every single detail of her life in explicit detail, until he runs out of time on the date. Because she is *too* open, the guy will never become interested in the deeper levels of commitment with her.

She is predictable and boring, kind of like the female version of the "nice guy." As such, she usually ends up being ghosted especially if someone who has the "mystery" element comes along.

## STAGNATING AND NEVER EVOLVING

This is a woman who has been left by her husband after years of marriage. Because constant evolution is an element that manifests itself continuously over longer periods of time, it's also the hardest one to reveal when it's missing. As such, someone missing this element might take years before they hit rock bottom in their slow slide away from romantic attachment.

In many ways, a lack of personal growth is boredom in its nastiest form. It is prolonged, dripping itself one inch at a time, until the glass is full (and that's when the relationship implodes).

Women missing out on this element will very commonly find themselves feeling lost at some point. Life is meant to be enjoyed and explored, and with that comes new knowledge and evolution. However, the woman who is missing out on her "constant evolution" element doesn't get the taste of that; moreover, she realizes it too late, as if she is the girl who didn't graduate with her friends and has to spend the summer studying instead of playing.

All of these are, of course, *examples* of what could happen, and they only scratch the surface of the issue. They are also scenarios where only one of the "iceberg" elements is missing. Each time a new, additional element is missing, the problems become even more complex.

The good news about all this is that you can diagnose the problem and become a much more fulfilled person *before* you meet a special someone. None of these elements are unattainable (not in the slightest bit). They are all things you can work on. They are all things that can become part of you—not because you want to use them in your dating life, but because they actually improve the quality of your life before you even start dating someone new!

# AFTERWORD

Nothing breaks like a heart, say Miley Cyrus and Mark Ronson from my Spotify playlist (Ronson & Cyrus, 2018).

Indeed, nothing breaks like hearts do. And even more so, nothing breaks like women's hearts do. Hit after hit, women band-aid their hearts into oblivion and bitterness. Men walk into their lives, men walk out—and all women are left with is sheer emptiness.

This is not to say that men don't get hurt. Oh, they do! This is not about the "battle of sexes," or how men are supposedly inherently inclined to hurt women. This is about the different shades of pain women have to bear with them, one after the other.

Whatever happened to you, regardless of whether you ended a relationship a month, a year, or a decade ago, and even if you have never been in one, it's time to stop the cycle. Your hurting will hurt you and others. End the pattern by embracing your Brilliant Vixen and attracting the very best the Universe has to give you.

Because the world, the Universe, the clouds, and the entire "species" of men are not to blame for your pain. Your conjecture is to blame, maybe. And maybe, to some extent, you are to blame for falling into the same pattern over and over again. Without a doubt, society and the expectations imposed on you as a woman have had a very big role to play in all this.

You can tear yourself apart from this and embrace a life that gives you nothing but joy, and not just in terms of dating. You can find yourself and fall in love with yourself again and again and again before you meet the one man who'll be the one who deserves to stand by your side as you joyfully conquer the world together.

It all starts with being the kind of woman these men are looking for, but even more than that, it all starts with being the kind of woman you want to be, however you define that.

The Brilliant Vixen model is only a blueprint: you get to fill in the empty spaces between the major pillars drawn in this book. You choose what type of fun you are, or how you feed your mystery, for example. You choose how you mirror your high-value. And you choose the specific terms in which you define each and every element in the Brilliant Vixen iceberg.

What is important to keep in mind is that each and every element presented in this book is **essential**. You can have one, two, or six of them—if you don't have all seven, you don't have the Brilliant Vixen approach, and you are likely to fall into the same pattern that hurt you the first, second, and third time around.

As mentioned in the introduction, I do not claim to hold the ultimate truth. I have, however, studied human behavior quite a bit, and I know that everything in this book is tried and tested (on me and other people whom I have helped over the years).

I also know women are absolutely amazing and they deserve men who are just as great as they are. *YOU* deserve to be with a man who values you for the best you offer this world, for a man who finds you not only attractive and fun, but also smart, incredible, and mysterious even after years and years of being together.

You deserve a man who wants to make you happy in the bedroom as much as he wants to make you happy everywhere outside of the bedroom. A man who respects who you are precisely because you are amazing from every point of view. A man who knows that no other woman on Earth could ever offer him what you have.

I trust that all the advice in this book will help you get there, but I do not want you to take these Brilliant Vixen stages as a way to get a man only. In fact, I would love for you to find your best self and your true sense of happiness. I truly hope this helps you find the ideal life you have in your heart and mind.

Finding a man is never a Brilliant Vixen's sole purpose in life. Her goal is to continuously find herself and better herself in all aspects. She wants to be fun and flirty, she is genuine down to every cell in her body, she wants to show her high value, she wants to be a challenge (and be challenged in a beautiful way), she wants to be a mystery, and she wants to be a work of art she continuously chisels down to the smallest detail.

Finding a man should never be your main drive.

You should be your main drive. Because you are the one piloting your body and your mind and taking them to new horizons in your love life and outside of it. When you finally understand that you want to be amazing not for men, but for your own happiness, great men will also start chasing you.

The entire process of unveiling your Brilliant Vixen should not be a chore. It should be a journey of self-discovery and self-love, a way to find your path and draw it in whatever colors you want. When you nail that, dating will be fun and the heartache cycle will finally end.

People come and go. Men come and go. You stay. From the moment you are born to the moment you leave Earth, you are the steadiest rock in your life. Rely on yourself, rather than men and silly dating advice, and you will win, not only in dating, but in life as well.

You see, nobody can give you a secret recipe for happiness. Nobody can dictate what you do with your body, who you date, or how many mistakes you make along the way. We all make them, but there comes a time in the life of every man and woman when the pattern of heartache has to stop.

And it all begins with you pushing the refresh button to yourself. You might not believe it fully right now, but you really have it in you to be the kind of "femme fatale" men chase, adore, and love for the rest of their lives. It doesn't matter what size you are, how blond or brunette your hair is, or how much experience you have in the bedroom. What truly matters is how you perfect yourself, both intellectually and physically.

When I started writing this book, I wanted to reach out to as many women as possible. I knew the depth of heartache because, like you, I have been hurt one too many times. It took me a while to understand that I cannot wait for whatever version of Fate to throw me a good life, but that I have to go out and take it.

Which is exactly what I did and exactly what I hope you will do as well. Put a smile on your face and learn how to be fun, learn how to flirt with grace and femininity, learn how to be sincere, and learn how to show men and everyone else that you're more than all that. Learn how to continuously stir up the challenging factor and the mystery in your relationship. But more than anything, learn how to never stagnate as a person.

The power to do all this lies within you. Go out and get it. Be the happiness magnet you were always meant to be!

With much love,

*Victoria Knightley*

# FREE GIFT FOR MY READERS

**Free Gift For My Readers!**

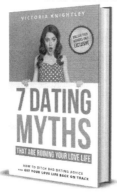

Do you know the most common and hurtful dating myths out there?

The things that are just ruining your love life?

If you want to learn more about the 7 most common myths putting a halt on your happiness, enjoy this FREE GIFT!

Scan the QR code above with your smartphone or tablet

If you want to learn more about the 7 most common myths putting a halt on your happiness, enjoy this FREE GIFT FOR MY READERS!

# REFERENCES

*A quote by C.G. Jung.* (n.d.-a). Goodreads.com. https:// www.goodreads.com/quotes/50795-i-am-not-what- happened-to-me-i-am-what

*A quote by C.G. Jung.* (n.d.-b). Goodreads.com. Retrieved 8 September 2020, from https://www. goodreads.com/quotes/75948-the-privilege-of-a- lifetime-is-to-become-who-you

*A quote by Dale Carnegie.* Goodreads.com. Retrieved 8 September 2020, from https://www.goodreads.com/ quotes/1140103-inaction-breeds-doubt-and-fear- action-breeds-confidence-and-courage

A quote by (Glasser, 2001) Glasser, W. (2001). *Choice theory: a new psychology of personal freedom.* Harper- perennial.

*A quote by Jonathan Heatt*. Goodreads.com. https://www.goodreads.com/quotes/7220106-i-had-too-much-fun-was-no-one-s-last-regret

Aristotle. *Aristotle quotes*. BrainyQuote. https://www.brainyquote.com/quotes/aristotle_379604

Baltatescu, S. (2014). Psychological distance. *Encyclopedia of Quality of Life and Well-Being Research*, 5145–5146. https://doi.org/10.1007/978-94-007-0753-5_2306

Barker, E. (2014). *Science of sexy: 5 things that can make you irresistible*. Time. https://time.com/2859728/science-of-sexy-5-things-that-can-make-you-irresistible/

Geher, G. (2013). *Mating intelligence unleashed: The role of the mind in sex, dating, and love*. Choice Reviews Online, 51(02), 51-1173-51-1173. https://doi.org/10.5860/choice.51-1173

Hardy, B. (2015). *20 signs you've evolved as a person*. Observer. https://observer.com/2015/12/20-signs-youve-evolved-as-a-person/

Hays, K., Thomas, O., Maynard, I., & Bawden, M. (2009). The role of confidence in world-class sport performance. *Journal Of Sports Sciences*, 27(11), 1185-1199. https://doi.org/10.1080/02640410903089798

Hopper, E. (2018). Healthy Psych. https://healthypsych.com/the-study-of-authenticity/

Jung, C. (2011). *Your vision will become clear only when you can look into your own heart. Who looks outside, dreams; who looks inside, awakes.* Philosiblog. https://philosiblog.com/2011/09/05/your-vision-will-become-clear-only-when-you-can-look-into-your-own-heart-who-looks-outside-dreams-who-looks-inside-awakes/

Kierkegaard, S. *Soren Kierkegaard quotes.* BrainyQuote. https://www.brainyquote.com/quotes/soren_kierkegaard_414008

Macmillan. (2020). Macmillan Dictionary. Macmillandictionary.com. https://www.macmillandictionary.com/

Maraboli, S. (2009). Life, the Truth, and Being Free (1st ed.). A Better Today Publishing.

Park, L., Young, A., & Eastwick, P. (2015). (Psychological) Distance makes the heart grow fonder. *Personality And Social Psychology Bulletin*, 41(11), 1459-1473. https://doi.org/10.1177/0146167215599749

Ronson, M., & Cyrus, M. (2018). *Nothing Breaks Like a Heart* [Streamed]. Sony Music Entertainment. https://www.youtube.com/watch?v=A9hcJgtnm6Q

Rougemont, D. (1995). Love in the Western world. Princeton University Press.

Smith, J. (2019). Twitter. Twitter.com. https://twitter.com/judahsmith/status/1093970239736418304?lang=en

Taylor, T. (2010). *Why mystery matters*. Psychologies. https://www.psychologies.co.uk/self/why-mystery-matters.html

Wade, T., & Feldman, A. (2016). Sex and the perceived effectiveness of flirtation techniques. *Human Ethology Bulletin*, 31(2), 30-44. https://doi.org/10.22330/heb/312/030-044

Welch, R. *Raquel Welch quote*. Quotefancy.com. https://quotefancy.com/quote/1592800/Raquel-Welch-You-know-what-s-the-sexiest-thing-of-all-A-little-mystery

Galoustian, G. (2020). *Being fun is no laughing matter*. ScienceDaily. https://www.sciencedaily.com/releases/2020/04/200423093725.htm

Printed in Great Britain
by Amazon